RIVER JOURNEYS

RIVER JOURNEYS

RUSSELL BRADDON · CHRISTINA DODWELL · GERMAINE GREER
WILLIAM SHAWCROSS · BRIAN THOMPSON · MICHAEL WOOD

HIPPOCRENE BOOKS, NEW YORK

Picture credits

COLOUR: BBC below p. 163; BBC/Clive Syddall both p. 61, top p. 62; BBC/David Wallace all pp. 25–28, 97–104, 137, both p. 140, top p. 141 and both p. 144; BBC/Christopher Warren all p. 197, both p. 198, top p. 199; Sonia Halliday p. 199; Dr A. Mountjoy top p. 162; Photographic Library of Australia both p. 161, below p. 162, top p. 163 and p. 164; Spectrum Colour Library p. 200; South American Pictures both p. 138, p. 139, both p. 142 & p. 143. Pictures on pages 62, 63 & 64 were specially photographed for the BBC by Michael K. Nichols.

BLACK AND WHITE: Barnaby's Picture Library (G.R. Reitz) p. 183, (H. Kanus) p. 189, (Gerald Clyde) pp. 190 & 193, (Ken Lambert) p. 195; BBC pp. 149, 159 & 160; BBC/Clive Syddall pp. 49, 51, 54–56, both pp. 58 & 60, p. 74; BBC/David Wallace pp. 11, 14, 15, 17, 21, 22, 29, 34, 39, 41, 77, 79, 85, 86–88, 90, 93–95, 108, 111, 112, 113, 123, 124, 127, 129, 130, 131, 134 & 145; BBC/Christopher Warren p. 175; Camera Press (Matheson/BBC) p. 180, both p. 181, (Hilary MacLauglin) p. 202; Sonia Halliday p. 194; Dr A. Mountjoy p. 168; Photographic Library of Australia pp. 154, 169, 170 & 174; South American Pictures pp. 117, 121 & 132; Spectrum 203; Chris Webb pp. 157 & 158; Michael Wood pp. 42 & 44. Pictures on pp. 45, 70 & 73 were specially photographed for the BBC by Michael K. Nichols.

This edition published by Hippocrene Books, Inc.
171 Madison Avenue, New York, NY 10016, 1985
First published 1984 by the British Broadcasting Corporation
35 Marylebone High Street, London W1M 4AA

ISBN 0–87052–140–3

© The Contributors and the British Broadcasting Corporation 1984

Set in 10/13pt Monophoto Plantin Light and
printed in England by Jolly & Barber Limited, Rugby

CONTENTS

In the television series on which this book is based the principal members of the BBC crew were as follows.

THE CONGO
Director: David Wallace. Film Editor: Peter Rose. Music Composed by Terry Oldfield. Photography: David South. Sound Recordist: Michael Savage. Production Assistant: Janina Kolodziej.

THE MEKONG
Director: David Wallace. Film Editor: Graham Walker. Music Composed by Tim Souster. Photography: Alan Stevens. Sound Recordist: Geoff Tookey. Production Assistants: Lorelle Harker, Janina Kolodziej.

THE NILE
Director: Gerry Troyna. Film Editor: Pat Haggerty. Music Composed by Brian End. Photography: Colin Munn. Sound Recordist: Brian Showell. Production Assistant: Barbara Gibson.

THE SEPIK AND THE WAGHI
Director: Clive Syddall. Film Editor: Charles Davis. Music Composed by Alan Parker. Photography: Mike Sooner. Sound Recordist: David Brinicombe. Production Assistant: Lorelle Harker.

THE SÃO FRANCISCO
Director: David Wallace. Film Editor: Peter Rose. Music Composed by Howard Davison. Photography: Nigel Walters. Sound Recordist: Michael Turner. Production Assistant: Janina Kolodziej.

THE MURRAY
Director: Stafford Garner. Film Editor: Paul Cantwell. Music Composed by Cameron Allan. Photography: Michael Twemlow. Sound Recordist: John Garwood. Production Assistant: Carole Maccoll.

Graphic Design: Glen Carwithen.
Series Producers: Roger Laughton, David Wallace.

THE CONTRIBUTORS

RUSSELL BRADDON is Australian and was educated at Sydney University. He was taught by Japanese captors to build railway lines, aerodromes and tunnels during World War II and has eschewed all forms of manual labour ever since. He has written twenty-eight books, hundreds of feature articles, a play (which got excellent reviews but no audiences) and numerous radio and television scripts. He has also been doing the so-called 'lecture circuit' for years, has been a regular panellist on BBC's *Any Questions*, and returns to Australia whenever he finds life in London is making him too polished.

CHRISTINA DODWELL was born in Nigeria, West Africa, and educated in England. She worked in London as a secretary and interior designer. In 1975 she began a 20,000-mile journey through Africa, travelling by horse, camel and dugout canoe. Three years later she returned and in 1979 her first book, *Travels with Fortune*, was published. She gave a series of radio talks on BBC *Woman's Hour* and wrote articles for the *New Scientist*, before setting out to travel in Thailand and Papua New Guinea. It was a two-year journey, after which she lived in the USA and travelled in Central America. Her second book, *In Papua New Guinea*, was published in 1983, and her third, *An Explorer's Handbook*, in 1984. At present she is planning a visit to China.

GERMAINE GREER was born in Melbourne, Australia, in 1939, and educated at the Universities of Melbourne, Sydney and Cambridge. Her doctoral thesis was on Shakespeare's early comedies. Her first book was *The Female Eunuch*, published in 1970. Since then she has made many appearances on television, written for numerous periodicals and taught in British and American universities. In 1979 she published *The Obstacle Race: The Fortunes of Women Painters and their Work*. Her most recent book is *Sex and Destiny*, which was published in 1984. She has lived in the United Kingdom since 1964.

WILLIAM SHAWCROSS lives in London and is a writer and journalist. He has been writing about Indochina for many years. His book, *Sideshow; Kissinger, Nixon and the destruction of Cambodia*, was published in 1979, and in 1984 he published *The Quality of Mercy; Cambodia, Holocaust and Modern Conscience*.

BRIAN THOMPSON is a playwright and novelist. As well as writing many single plays for radio and television he has wide experience of making documentaries for the BBC. His sixth stage play, *Turning Over*, was seen at the Bush Theatre at the beginning of

1984. Its theme was the practice of documentary film-making. Brian Thompson has lived in Yorkshire, without a single regret, since 1961.

MICHAEL WOOD was born in Manchester and educated at Manchester Grammar School and at Oriel College, Oxford, where he read Modern History. He held undergraduate and postgraduate scholarships and in 1972 won the University's English Essay prize. His research work was in tenth-century history. Since 1976 he has worked for the BBC. He wrote and presented the *In Search of* . . . series and has written a book based on the programmes called *In Search of the Dark Ages*. He also wrote and presented one of the programmes in the series *Great Railway Journeys of the World* and contributed to a book which accompanied the series. Among his forthcoming publications is a full-length study of King Athelstan and his age, and a book which traces the development of Aegean archaeology, *In Search of the Trojan War*.

INTRODUCTION

'It's lovely to live on a raft,' said Huckleberry Finn as he drifted down his river, the Mississippi. 'We had the sky up there, all speckled with stars, and we used to lay on our backs and look up at them, and discuss whether they was made or only just happened.'

What could be better than a passage through today's world at a pace which offers time to reflect? But Mark Twain, more than anyone else, would have understood how different reality can be. As an apprentice pilot of a river-boat on the Mississippi, he knew all about the hazards which can beset the unwary.

When we decided to make a series of six films called *River Journeys*, we were following in the wake of some distinguished travellers. Mark Twain may have been the only river-boat man. But other writers like Graham Greene and Joseph Conrad have also found adventure and mystery on remote rivers. For the BBC, Michael Wood retraced Conrad's journey into the heart of Africa along the Zaïre River, known until modern times as the Congo, while Christina Dodwell's quest for excitement took her to the Waghi River in New Guinea. With a team of Californian adventurers, she attempted the first-ever passage of a hitherto uncharted river. Negotiating rapids on rubber rafts, with waves sometimes 25 feet high, Christina and the Americans experienced fear, exhilaration – and real danger. On one occasion three rafters were swept overboard. Two reached safety. The third was swept downriver for a quarter of a mile before he was thrown ashore out of sight and sound of his colleagues, half-drowned. The Waghi had lived up to its local nickname, 'The Eater of Men'.

Canoes, cargo-boats, ferries as big as towns, paddle-steamers. The writers in this anthology took their transport as it came. There was the paddle-steamer that limped upstream from Juàzeiro to Pirapora carrying Germaine Greer along the River São Francisco through Brazil's arid north-east. The boat was making its final trip before being reborn as a tourist attraction. It consumed forests of wood as it crept upriver. Crowds gathered to see it pass. Germaine Greer was not at all sure it would reach its destination. She was almost right. The boat reached Pirapora only to be destroyed by fire a few months later.

In Zaïre Michael Wood set off from Kinshasa on a huge boat which had its own police force, and was almost a city-state in its own right. Brian Thompson sent his letters home from the floating post office on the Nile penny boat as he passed through northern Sudan. Christina Dodwell travelled the first leg of her New Guinea journey in a Seventh-Day Adventist missionary boat, while Russell Braddon began his river journey in a canoe. A military patrol boat carried William Shawcross into Cambodia

9

as he made his way up the Mekong from Can Tho to Phnom Penh. There was the occasional tourist-boat too – on the Murray and on the Egyptian Nile. But, for the most part, these journeys were made where river transport is still the way people go from one place to another.

Of course, these travellers' tales are not just about boats and the people who travel on them. Germaine Greer is rightly more concerned about the decline of the River São Francisco than the demise of its namesake, the paddle-steamer on which she travelled. William Shawcross uses the opportunity of his unprecedented journey to examine the uneasy relationship between Vietnam and her neighbours. Russell Braddon rediscovers, through the tranquillity of the Murray River, lost feelings about his native land.

You will find no timetables here, no hints about how to avoid yellow fever. Even where two writers visit the same region – for Michael Wood and Brian Thompson both reached the watershed of Central Africa – you will find no common experience.

But these essays do proclaim one thing. It is still possible, as the jumbo jets wing overhead, for the independent traveller to find places where the tourists do not go. It is still possible to meet people who know nothing of the issues which divide the planet. It is still possible to be enveloped by the pace and peace of a great river.

> 'The moment that the boat was under way in the river, she was under the sole and unquestioned control of the pilot. He could do with her exactly as he pleased, run her when and whither he chose, and tie her up to the bank whenever his judgement said that that course was best.'

That was Mark Twain again, describing life on the Mississippi when it was still a working river. Life on the Zaïre today isn't so very different.

> 'Whenever you leave Kinshasa, you do what you want. There's nobody to tell you that you can't do this or you can't do that. You're free.'

That was François, once skipper of a Rhine barge, now piloting a cargo-boat between Kinshasa and Kisangani. Lucky man.

Roger Laughton, Executive Producer, March 1984.

THE CONGO

Michael Wood

Going up that river was like travelling back to the earliest beginnings of the world when vegetation rioted on the earth and the big trees were kings. An empty stream, a great silence, an impenetrable forest . . . you thought yourself bewitched and cut off forever from everything you had known once – somewhere – far away – in another existence perhaps.

Joseph Conrad, *Heart of Darkness*

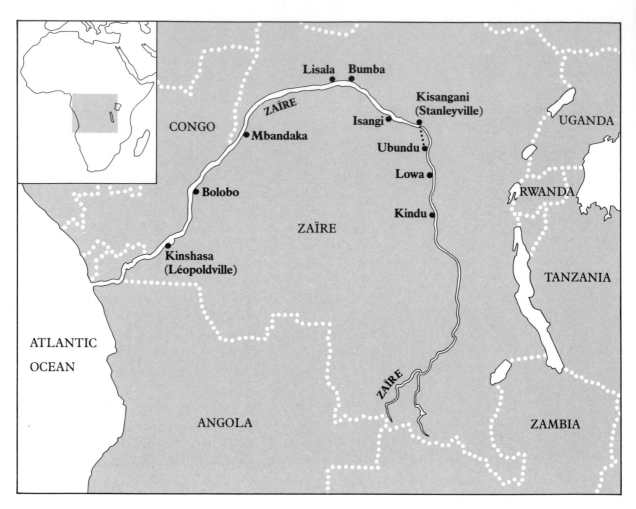

PART ONE: THE *KOKOLO*

'Will I be able to contact your embassy for help if I get into trouble?'

The ambassador's face wrinkled with amusement. 'You must be joking. You'll be on your own, chum. I'm afraid that's the answer to that question. Once you're upriver, communication with the outside world, or even within Zaïre, is virtually impossible, unless you come across a mission station with a radio. It's best to be self-sufficient, take your own medicines, malaria pills, water-purifying tablets and so on.' (I had.) 'The river-water is only safe to drink after you've filtered and boiled or purified it, but it's perfectly safe to swim in: just the odd crocodile or hippo to look out for, and they can be very nasty customers – a hippo with young is to be avoided at all costs.' (Was he having me on?)

The ambassadorial Jaguar slowed to walking pace, its air-conditioning a barely audible hum, as it met the teeming crowds outside the dock gates. The epitome of the laconic and imperturbable British diplomat abroad, HM Ambassador to the Republic of Zaïre, formerly the Belgian Congo, paused for a serious reflection.

'It's important to realise that Africa is different. The people you will meet upriver have their own view of the world. They live for the day, they accept death as a daily part of life, they are closer to nature and to the family than we are, they have a resignation and an amazing patience which we in the West have quite lost. You must try to see it through their eyes.'

The car stopped. We shook hands.

'Well, there we are: best of luck . . . almost wish I was coming with you.'

The electric window closed soundlessly and the car was gone. I was swept towards the gangplank by a wave of people, jostled against panniers of smoked monkey, a monstrous catfish, bottles of palm-oil, baskets of bread; a dead antelope over a man's shoulder, its mouth flecked with foam and blood, left red specks on my shirt. At the quay edge I could see the river running high, covered with bobbing clumps of vegetation borne down from the rain forests of the heart of Africa; opposite, an island with the half-submerged wrecks of old river-steamers, their spindly funnels silhouetted in the lowering sun. It was five o'clock; the boat left at six, the crowds were gathering and I felt a little dizzy with this first taste of the raw vitality of the river life. And that smell! Wafting across the turbid, tea-coloured current: sweet, hot, ripe. Is it the vegetation? The red soil? The piles of rubbish smoking on every corner? The skin and sweat of the people themselves? It first hits you, with that wall of heat, when you step out of the plane door at Ndjili, when in a second your shirt is soaked and you feel light-headed. It is forever the smell of Africa. You never forget it.

The boat is there. Moored to the quay, several decks rising above the throng. Huge barges are being pulled in front by tugs. Time to find my cabin.

Strange how many writers have already, in such a comparatively short time, written books about this journey, conspiring to make it a mythic voyage, turning it into a metaphor. The river has fascinated people as a snake would a bird (I borrow Conrad's phrase) and the snake has charmed them. Most of all, of course, it is Conrad. His nightmare vision of his own journey up the Congo (on which he nearly died) fascinated me too, long before I ever went there. The journey, however, is not an ancient one, though it is already charged with potent memories. The Portuguese were the first Europeans in modern times to see the mouth of the second greatest river in the world, in 1482, but over 200 miles of rapids presented an impassable barrier to exploration, and it was only in 1877 that H. M. Stanley became the first person to travel the length of the Congo. That was at the time of the scramble for Africa, and in Stanley's wake came the imperialists, the profiteers, planters and exploiters, as the Belgian river-steamers opened up this trade route into the heart of what Europeans liked to think of as the Dark Continent. Then this vast country, the size of western Europe, was the private slave empire of Léopold, king of the Belgians, and it was then that the journey and its terrors inspired that twentieth-century masterpiece *Heart of Darkness* (published in 1902). Now the white epoch, Conrad's 'fantastic invasion', has receded, and though much of Africa is still in economic thrall to the western world, we can only be grateful that so much of Africa has survived the burden of the white man. I travelled on the river twice between late March and mid-June 1982, armed with some money, some medicines, a mosquito net, and my schooldays' French (all of them essential, I might add). I got 1300 miles by river from Kinshasa, as far as Kindu, where the second long navigable stretch ends.

All travellers must start at Kinshasa (Léopoldville), already 300 miles from the sea. In the old days you sailed from Antwerp (Conrad's 'sepulchral city') to Matadi in the estuary, or took the service which still runs from Marseilles via Conakry, Grand Bassam, Grand Popo, and Cotonou, a journey told by Gide in his *Journey to the Congo* and made memorable by Céline in *Journey to the End of the Night*. Modern travellers, who generally have little time (or patience) for long sea voyages, will probably fly in, as I did, to the new airport of Ndjili and take a taxi on to Kinshasa and to the Memling Hotel, last of the colonial hotels of Léopoldville (where incidentally Graham Greene stayed in search of his Burnt-Out Case). From Kinshasa the big boats go up most Monday nights. Kinshasa used to be the port for the whole of the Belgian Congo, and the river is still the great artery of communication within Zaïre, as few can afford plane flights and there are no good roads into the interior (the Belgians left surprisingly little). But few foreigners come here today, still less to travel up the great river: in all my weeks on it I never met another white traveller going by boat. The story of my journey is told from notes I made at the time, with excerpts from a detailed diary I kept from Mbandaka onwards.

The *Kokolo* is one of the great boats of the world. Not on the Ganges, the Mississippi or the Amazon will you encounter such a boat. A huge, six-decked steamer which pushes five, six, or even more barges ahead of it: two-storey barges on which hundreds of people live for the nine days it takes to reach Kisangani. Tonight ours is carrying 1500 people, but they sometimes take up to 4000, especially on the Kasai (a tributary of the Congo), when it is standing room only even on the roofs of the barges. The buyers and sellers spend their year going up and downriver; you will see them putting

The *Kokolo* leaving Kinshasa. Right: preparing food on one of the *Kokolo*'s barges

their panniers down in the queue for the return trip as soon as they dock in Kisangani. The merchants are mainly women; most live and sleep on the deck with their piles of wares, the better-off rent the rough cabins on the barges and keep their animals tethered there, sleeping against the door. If the animals die en route they smoke them there and then; in the absence of refrigeration they have even been known to throw them into the water on a line and tow them behind the boat! The *Kokolo*, then, is a floating town full of smells and noise, vice and commerce. But above all, commerce. Most people travel purely to sell.

Needless to say, whites don't travel on these boats, even first class. It is unheard of to see them on the barges. But the barges are the centre of life on the boat. At night the alleyways are lit by oil-lamps and packed with people and their goods. Walking down among them you pass piles of fabrics, second-hand clothes, panniers of smoked fish, you bump into live animals – you might tread on a muzzled crocodile in the gloom! In big enamel basins are heaps of VD antibiotics, razor-blades, marijuana, cassettes, biros, grubs, manioc 'flour' wrapped in leaves, smoked bats. In the 'streets', which bear names such as 'rue Budja', people meet and talk. At night there are many places where you can go to gamble and have a drink, but on the upper deck of the Budja barge there is an open space with tables and benches where crowds gather and dance to a cranky little disco from an old record-player in a nearby cabin, the speaker cones facing down on empty oil-drums to get the necessary volume. The music itself is Zaïrean, Cameroon, Nigerian highlife, Kenyan, reggae of course (Bob Marley is a symbol of black pride in much of the Third World), even western pop – 'By the Rivers of Babylon' rang out as we floated through Stanley Pool that first night.

A first-class ticket on the *Kokolo* gives you a cabin with bathroom, breakfast (tea or coffee, bread and jam), lunch (say, soup, fish, manioc and vegetables) and dinner (perhaps meat or chicken, or omelettes, pineapple or tapioca). This way you travel in relative comfort. The boat continues all night, so you have no need of your mosquito nets (the breeze keeps the mosquitoes off) though there is no air-conditioning and the heat is sometimes tremendous.

There were memorable scenes: such as the morning when hundreds of pirogues (dugout canoes) came paddling out into the pool of Bolobo bearing monkeys, manioc and bananas, the fruits of the forest, to be bartered for the baubles and drugs piled in the stinking alleys of the *Kokolo*; but none more memorable than when the sky goes black and a tropical storm thrashes across the glassy surface of the river, with the traders rushing frantically to pack their precious goods into boxes; the silvery light when the sky clears, and the breeze carries the smell of the sodden forest, fecund, warm and ripe. It was on such a day, in the aftermath of such a storm, that I heard beautiful plainsong from the bow of the Budja barge. Some Christians, Kimbanguists, had gathered together in the well-deck to sing hymns in Lingala, the river language. With descants weaving round it like bluebirds, the name of Jesus floated across the mirror of the stream, resounding in a deep male resonance while pirogues slowly pulled away and fell behind. Businessmen and politicians, the only ones with money, may fly over Africa from city to city in air-conditioned jumbo jets. This is what they never see or experience.

Villagers come to trade with the *Kokolo* in their pirogues

The *Kokolo* is an easy enough way to get up to Kisangani; the heat is the only real discomfort. But I wanted to go by a variety of boats, and I decided to break my journey four days out at Mbandaka. Here I left the *Kokolo* and struck out on my own. You approach Mbandaka along the southern bank past tall trees which lean over the river, past the wrecks of old river-steamers, past the twin-towered church and its giant palm-trees: it is heart-stoppingly beautiful, and now I can never think of it without a terrible feeling of longing. I cannot explain why. It must be that with its smells, its tall trees, its decaying buildings, its peculiar accident of position, Mbandaka produces a feeling of forgetfulness in me such as do certain drugs in myths. And yet what is the place really? A steamy river-station with a dirty port. Rubbish, grounded barges, wrecks, old tramps, brick warehouses, painted mansions faded and crumbling. Red-soil streets. The vegetation is especially lush: just above the junction of the Ubangi and the Congo, dead on the equator, we are surrounded by the tropical rain forest which borders the river for the next 1000 miles.

After the departure of the *Kokolo*, I took a *pousse-pousse* down the river-bank to find a room. The hotel was built in the early fifties, a period of great confidence, but unbeknown to them all too close to the fall, the sudden abandonment of the Congo by the Belgians in 1959. You approach it from the road along the river, past a row of enormous palms. At the entrance, set in the floor in black-and-white mosaic, you read 'Bienvenu: Hôtel Afrique'. This is the 'vieil hôtel du fleuve'. Inside the reception is a fine polished wood counter, its pillars hung with old posters, faded and tattered, celebrating the foundation of Air Zaïre, or Lake Kivu. On the wall by the marble staircase is a great framed map of Congo Belge on which – the porter proudly points out – Mbandaka is still called Coquilhatville. What a lovely name. Sounds gay and light, suggests jacarandas and coquetry, flowers of desire that sting the heart. (In fact, the reality was far more prosaic: Coquilhat was the Belgian founder of the town.) An old fan turns slowly in the high ceiling. Cobwebs on the key-boxes.

'No, you don't want to stay here, monsieur, there is a much better hotel up the road, built recently with all the facilities.'

'Can't I stay here?'

'Not really. Try the new hotel.'

'Go on.'

'No, the new hotel is better for you.'

'But I like buildings like this.'

Eventually he relents. The rooms are like pre-war flats: iron bedstead, old mattress; an old cupboard, tiled floor, with a communal loo and water-tap down a long, dark corridor. Faded black-and-white western pin-up in a wooden stand on the sideboard; another on the wall, a grotesque caricature with blonde hair and pouting lips: so that's what the vieil hôtel has come to. It's the river-traders' whorehouse! In the huge restaurant bar – where now no meal is ever cooked – sit a couple of sultry and surly girls in the long black cotton Zaïrean 'abacos', sipping warm beer. 'Bonjour citoyennes. . .'

The bar opens onto a crumbling terrace with big palms and bougainvillaea. The view over the river is breathtaking. To the left, downstream, old river-steamers with their black-and-white funnels lie grounded and rotting, tendrils of the forest snaking through their wheel-house windows; upstream, families are washing their linen at the water's edge on a ruined barge, their home. The river is running full and high, dotted with bobbing, bottle-green islands of water hyacinths, some blooming blue flowers; on the other bank a village on stilts; opaque, silvery light, pirogues gently moving upstream, voices hanging in the still air, carrying far across the water; an old stern-wheeler makes its way slowly upstream leaving a trail of black smoke, the blades of its paddle-wheel thumping into the eddying current. A place to contemplate. I soon fell in love with lovely old Mbandaka, steamy, overripe, its colonial façades crumbling, its white opulence long since taken back by Africa. I can understand why Greene's Burnt-Out Case came here to find himself. Go to Africa to cure a sick heart: that's what they used to say. But the river drew me back.

Getting the next boat upstream was not quite as easy as that, however. There was no state passenger-boat going upriver for ten days; of the smaller privately owned transports no one could say anything, and there were none in the port. I could, however, try to hitch a lift with a cargo captain, if he was willing. The boat was called *Nkoy* ('Leopard') 7 and the captain had the very English-sounding name of Philips.

PART TWO: *NKOY 7*

Wednesday 24 March. Our captain arrives. A red-haired, freckled, stocky, tough Fleming. His name is François Philips. He speaks fast and vigorous French. A former Rhine boatman, he is out here on a two-year contract (paid in Belgian francs). Seems happy enough to have me on board, if a bit offhand: shrugs shoulders and gestures with Popeye ham-bone arms.

'Well, if the *chef de zone* agrees then you can come along.'

'Is there a cabin?'

'Yes, one: that's mine. If you want to come you'll have to sleep on the deck.'

My enquiry about food was greeted just as uncompromisingly. He has an improvised freezer cooled by a fan run off the generator, but the meat in it is his; likewise the bread, butter, salt, sugar. 'It's calculated for my journey, I haven't food for a second person. You must get your own.'

(God, I thought, where in Mbandaka do I get food for a long journey? And *what* do I buy? A crate of bananas? A goat?! Or the stuff I saw on the decks of the *Kokolo*?)

'Go and see Stephane: he's a good butcher, he'll sort you out with meat and groceries. You'll have to allow a good ten days from here to Kisangani, fourteen to be safe: we'll have a lot to do in Mobeka, Lisala, at Bumba, Mombongo, Basoko, and each one will take a day.'

I felt a thrill of excitement as he rattled off this litany of mysterious names, picturing villages on stilts under a gloomy canopy of rain forest, haunt of mantises and snakes – or will they be bustling ports like Mbandaka? Captain Philips turned away and climbed the ladder to the bridge.

'We leave at dawn – between five and six.'

Thursday 25 March. Five o'clock or so. I walk down to the Congo with my bags. This is the best time of the day in Africa. A refreshing breeze, the smell of dying wood-fires and overripe vegetation, the mauve light. Dawn rises fast, a few minutes. I come to the Congo itself and walk upstream along the bank. There I pass the large buildings of a great mission station, the second biggest in the country. There is a big, red-brick basilica with twin towers, and other large buildings with long verandas and shutters, once brightly painted, their stucco now faded and crumbling.

Everywhere there are elegant buildings seemingly no longer in use, closed. A marvellous villa in a walled garden, with side loggias on the first floor, long french windows and venetian blinds, shaded by an overhanging roof. A place of elegance and civilisation. Once the home of a rich man, who held *soirées* and *thés dansants*.

The gardens are overgrown – returning to Africa. In a hundred years it will need an archaeologist (or a poet) to piece together the story of what must have been a vast investment of men and materials. It was a time when men of the church and of commerce hacked out these outposts of civilisation deep in the Dark Continent, keeping contact through the daily papers, the weekly post, the regular steamers. A time when the missions believed unswervingly in their civilising power – and their power to save souls; when the administrators had no doubts that they could bring Europeans to Africa and 'make it work'.

But this is still a working mission. On the dawn wind come first the beats of drums, isolated and muffled; then the deep tones of male voices. As you pass the church, you see there are still buildings of the mission kept up, with clean-swept courtyards and flower-beds, and you soon hear the full, swelling tones of a male choir singing the Lord's praises to the beat of the African tom-tom. Outside the sky is lightening to a reddish-mauve, the wind gently touching the giant palms which line the road.

At the boat I say my goodbyes to another captain, André, who is going downstream. 'I fell asleep fully clothed, only woke up at four o'clock.' They had been hitting wine and whisky after at least a dozen large bottles of beer each. 'I wish you were travelling with me – I could show you something: this place is going down and down, and will not come back up. The two years of my contract and I am off – pouff – back to Belgium. You'll see.'

We push away from the jetty, churning up the mat of *jacinthes d'eau* (water hyacinths). The river seems to flow imperceptibly (actually its current is very strong). A journey of ten days is beginning.

A steady, slow progress upriver, pushing against a powerful current. The occasional pirogue comes to sell fish or fruit to the crewmen who are quartered on our bow. One comes out from the tiny fishing village of Neganda, a seasonal place, a *village des riverains*, of thatches and straw, with wicker brakes, on the edge of one of the islands in midstream, half-hidden in the dense jungle which lines our route. Mostly we can only see one bank, or even neither, as we negotiate a path gingerly between islands in a river sometimes 10 miles wide.

We had not found a suitable berth at six, and François decided to press on for over an hour, navigating by the flash of an electrical storm and the beam of his lights. An extraordinary scene this: the lamplight flashing into the deep night to port, illuminating the jungle to starboard; streams of moths and other insects pouring into the light; the black night; the horizon lit up with lightning from miles away; the silvery flashes on the slowly swirling water.

In the meantime I prepared some steak, potatoes and peas, for François and me. We drank a bottle of Portuguese wine with it, too, and chatted till ten-thirty or so. Then, having made my bed on the deck, a torrential storm forced me to pull the mosquito net inside; and I slept on the floor of the bridge indoors, which was hot (and some mosquitoes had evidently taken refuge there from the storm – I was bitten).

Friday 26 March. We were up for dawn. I feel pretty terrible: the motor runs all night, vibrating through the deck. I expect I shall get used to it. François came on the bridge at five o'clock and we were slowly moving upstream soon after. By sixish the pirogues were with us. Throughout the voyage, buying and selling takes place.

Five-thirty. All day the boat has pushed along, making its eight knots against the thick, powerful, flowing stream – a swelling, eddying, brown flow, dotted with islands of vegetation. It is the path of the weed and hyacinths which the steersman follows, for the channels themselves change sometimes week by week as the myriad tributaries of the Congo pour their contents into the great flood and shift its sandy shoals.

Michael Wood peeling potatoes on *Nkoy 7*

The sky was a uniform grey, cloudy, and admitting no direct sunlight, stifling and heavy. Lunch, with its cold beers, came as a blessed relief. François shared his pan of home-made tomato soup, and with my bread, cheese, jambon fumé, salami and pieces of papaya, we ate well. We felt desperate for a siesta, but so hot and windless was the air that even lying on the open deck brought little relief. Still we dozed fitfully till about three-thirty-five, when a great commotion arose.

We were nearing a native village where the boys expected to do well *avec le commerce*. And sure enough, even more than in the morning, pirogue after pirogue crossed our wake, bearing goods to sell. Some of them had filled with water as the men struggled to get a mooring-line aboard, some were lost altogether and fell back into our wake, the women shrieking, while our boys roared with laughter. The visitors carried their produce onto the deck – smoked steaks of crocodile meat, parts of legs and tail (the greatest delicacy, a light white meat), panniers of smoked monkeys, trussed up together, blackened like wizened little babies, their arms up in a foetal position; tortoises; fine big fish (manganza); a 3-foot catfish; bags of fat, live grubs for frying; the interminable panniers of smoked fish; live cocks and geese. Soon the pirogues are four deep in places; the decks are dotted with women in bright, cotton print frocks, carrying their kids papoose-style, their marvellous, spiky hair-dos like radar antennae; the men fingering the smoked fish suspiciously – our boys, after all, have the upper hand in the bargaining – there may be no other boat for days.

Villagers in pirogues alongside *Nkoy 7* try to sell a monkey to the crew

(François bought three manganza for 40Z this morning – the seller wanted 60.) The tortoises are tethered to iron stanchions – those for slaughter – while another big tortoise is left in the water which was gathered last night in the lifeboat.

François decides to kill the bigger one here and now and put its meat in the freezer. The scene is astonishing: François hacking and cutting at a feverish speed, as if trying to get his gruesome task – effectively skinning the creature alive – over and done with. The tortoise's strength and toughness, resisting even when François, helped by Kalala and his cook, has opened up the shell and entirely cut the shell away from the muscled tissue. Finally they force its head out of the folds of flesh and François stabs in a knife, pinions it to the improvised block, and strikes with a great machete. It takes a dozen or more ferocious blows before the animal gives up and its head is severed, its shell long since thrown into the water. Yellow eggs spill out. It was a female. Its heart still pumps. This is life on the river. Out of it everyone takes food and makes commerce.

After all that I take a shower in river-water. My skin feels prickly and stretched, but at the same time sweaty and clogged. The shower is terrific and I come out a new man. Better still, a gentle, fresh wind has come up, the sky lightening to blue ahead of us; the last hour of daylight is pleasant: standing on the deck in a towel, hair dripping; the warm, refreshing wind wafts the rich, 'living' smell of the forest: it feels good to be alive. The boys are done with the commerce for today and some are stretched on the hold covers; François is cutting up the tortoise, whose claw still momentarily grips him. From here to Lisala and beyond, the commerce will be heavy: this is pretty much how we will spend the next few days. Same commerce, same heat, and above all, same river.

It's five to six. We have no yard-arm, but I have decided that the sun touches it at six o'clock, when we can have the first beer of the evening. The boat is slowing. Another night *en pleine brousse*! Must get the mosquito net up now before the insects take over the night.

Saturday 27 March. It is ten-thirty a.m. and today has already been eventful. I rose at five-thirty, half an hour before dawn, and the boat was on the move soon after. The morning was surprisingly chill. Pirogues came very early with their wares, some failing to negotiate a rather choppy surface and missing us altogether. At around six-thirty there was a sudden juddering jar and the boat came to a halt close in at the end of an island. We had hit a sand-bar, right in the middle of the charted course.

François rushed onto the bridge, muttering, and one of the crew took soundings at the bow. The dozen or so piroguistes on the deck dived back into their boats, ready to push off in case violent motions capsized their precious cargoes. For a moment we stood on the bridge in silence as the engines rumbled, and François signalled reverse. A great eddy grew up on the starboard-midships, bringing up the red-brown sand and sediment from the river-bed. There seemed a chance we might be stuck, but presently the bows started to ease imperceptibly away to port – we were off. 'We could have been stuck here for at least four days, even a week,' said François, and then giggled as if that would have been a good joke.

The next half-hour or so was a matter of deliberately negotiating the old channel to the left bank, taking soundings every half-minute. There were no more alarms, and at eight-thirty we slowed and began to pull in to the left bank, where native huts could be seen. Two or three kilometres ahead, the spire of a church peered over the forest. We had arrived at the mission station and village of Makanza, formerly known as Nouvelle Anvers – New Antwerp – another of those fragile arrangements of familiarity made by colonists in foreign lands. We were to stop here for an hour while the crew went to the village market to get cooking oil for the galley. We tied up along a stretch of mud-flat and river-bank, lined by a dozen or more piroguistes, and I joined the boys in going ashore, stepping gingerly down the gangplank, trousers rolled above the knees to splash through the river to the bank.

We reached the market in a few minutes: a few rush-covered stalls with piles of manioc wrapped in palm-leaves, salt, some flour, home-made bread, biros, a few clothes, and not much else. No oil for the boys and I promise them one of the bottles I bought in Mbandaka, as we have been cooking with butter.

I was anxious to look at the mission station, for here at Makanza (so François had told me over dinner) was one of those Belgian priests who had got 'African fever'; a man who had come here in the twenties and was now eighty-two; one of those Europeans who go African in all but colour. Even the priests take women here; the Catholic authorities know, but turn a blind eye. Without drink and women in this heat, even a saint might find the Bible at times an insufficient comfort. But sixty years in this one place!

We walked along the dirt path in between shanties, thatched huts and palm-groves, the sky leaden, dull, but thankfully not burning hot. Ahead at the far end of this long approach parallel to the river was the imposing brick façade and spire of the church. A large dirt square lay in front, partly concreted around the steps. To the river side of the church a compound wall marked the mission enclosure, with several imposing buildings, including a verandaed house surrounded by palms.

We were immediately surrounded by a great crowd, mainly of children, and at the dispensary saw a number of mothers and babies – and the local doctor, white-coated, pleasant and very young. The priest was dead. He had still been alive at the celebrations of the station's centenary last year, but had since passed away and been buried in the mission cemetery in which he had walked and prayed for sixty years. When his type are finally gone, there will be none like them to stand in their place: of that much we can be sure.

As we walked to the church front, we heard tom-toms. No wonder those nineteenth-century explorers felt a *frisson* of fear! On entering the church we found, though, that these were for hymns. In a corner at the far end of the nave a crowd of young children suddenly started to sing Alleluia to an African rhythm and a tom-tom beat, conducted by their young black teacher (who sported a yellow 'Kiss' T-shirt!). What a sound! The sound of Africans singing the Lord's praises, echoing through the rafters of this great dusty old basilica with its painted plaster effigies of a white Virgin Mary; its great painting above the altar, showing a white Jesus; its decaying confessional stalls (are they still used?); its antiquated Belgian treadle organ with dilapidated lid, brass-bound stops and worn keys stained brown by a century of tropical heat and daily use. If Livingstone could come back now, would he take comfort in the 'success' of his beloved religion in Africa? Would he still have faith in its permanence? Come to think of it, would Stanley still feel the same confidence in the future which he displayed here 100 years ago? An African future shaped and directed by white skills, enterprise and will? White superiority? They would not believe what has happened and in so short a time.

Sunday 28 March. It is five a.m. I rose to the start of the ship's main engine. Feel grotty and puffy: right side of face looks like a boxer's, a swelling on the cheekbone, due to overexposure to a really burning sun when I was sitting reading on the deck yesterday. I put my T-shirt on and go down to the prow. Under my bare feet the iron deck is greasy with oil and the remains of smoked fish. It is cool, the river is dead flat, like glass or mother-of-pearl. Not the slightest shimmer on the surface. The sky is perfectly reflected in the water: a pale wash with a beautiful white and purple cloud formation upriver, faint bands of ultramarine and pink; to the north, over the forest,

Nkoy 7 at Bumba on the Zaïre River

Sunset, watched from *Nkoy 7*. Overleaf: a stern-wheel paddle-steamer hugging the bank of the Zaïre River

The fisheries at Wagania on the Zaïre river-banks

Michael Wood on the *Sarah*, sailing from Ubundu to Kindu

28

Dawn on board *Nkoy 7*. Michael Wood with the steersman

a cloudless sky with a single puff of purple. Where the sky meets the river in the distance a few low-flying islands float in a liquid haze. And there is the faintest breeze! Sometimes on the river, as now, or at sunset, the air blows so lightly, so gently, so voluptuously soft, that you imagine you could be breathing in deliciousness itself. This enchantment lasts only a moment. The sun appears ahead, just above the horizon, just behind a thin band of cloud. It is a clearly distinct, pale-red ball. As it moves higher, and you can watch it rise every second, it emerges from each belt of cloud brighter and whiter until it bursts out white-hot with a scorching halo illuminating our track upriver like moonlight. A wind comes up and ripples the whole river surface. Then the heat of the day begins.

Eight-thirty a.m. I'm feeling low physically. Sore throat (not serious says François; it's the river-water and he gets it himself). Also feel a bit feverish. Slight swollen gland in the groin, nothing to worry about yet. Slight eye infection which I treated with ointment and has now nearly gone. But hot and aching. Slept badly. Strange dreams.

The sun is now boiling hot, the sky blue and clear, and François has already forced a number of pirogue 'hitchhikers' away, by running his starboard-side along a great tree which had fallen in the stream. 'A dozen pirogues tied to us and we lose a kilometre an hour. They don't understand, you know. They're calling me *un blanc malin!*' He giggled hysterically. 'You can't hit them, you see. If a European hit them – pouff – it would be the end of the contract. But you can ask them a hundred times, and they would stand there and do nothing. So you must take the chance to get them off. But never show fear – if they learn you are frightened, you have had it.'

Six-thirty p.m. Just anchored 2°N 20.6°E near the outlet of River Eyole. A slothful Sunday. Had the last of the steak carbonnades with peas and home-made (by François) tomato consommé and Kivu white cabbage. Plus several beers.

Later in the afternoon pirogues came by off the island of Ukaturaka and some young men were ushered up to the cabin, bearing three enormous, heavy, incised copper amulet rings, of the kind formerly given by husbands to their bride-to-be and worn by the women forever as a sign of fidelity. François says they are hammered round the ankle and only taken off at death. The custom is now dead (says François) as of many years, and he thinks these could be as much as fifty years old. One is clearly old and damaged. The other two are massive and intact, obviously a matching pair, though differing in shape a little. 'No one out of the *brousse* knows how to make them any more,' says François. The copper comes from Katanga.

At six o'clock, just before we anchored, the lights loomed up of a great *pousseur*, the *Ngungu*, which swept past in the growing dark, illuminated from stem to stern, pushing its barges full of people, crammed in with their animals and belongings on the lower decks, the red lights of the bar on the upper decks, blasting rowdy chatter and music across the water. She flashed her headlights at us, and against the green backdrop of the rain forest, turning her searchlight on us as she passed downstream, her wake glittering as bright as day. A city passing in the night! The stench of cooking, animals, urine and excrement drifted over the river and lingered for a while after she vanished.

Now, at seven-thirty, I'm sitting at the table with François, having yet another beer (thank God it is not very alcoholic!).

Monday 29 March. Up at five-thirty. Marvellous, flat, early light – monochrome, the river like glass. Problems even before breakfast. We see a *pousseur* anchored close upriver and a cargo-boat further up. We move forward and we hit sand. The channel is sanded and all three ships are stopped. Consternation on the bridge: involved shouting with piroguistes – do they know where the channel might be? Eventually the farther one of the two boats upstream detaches its load and, lightened considerably, edges across to ascertain a channel. He turns and we follow him back. An hour lost – but should still make the rocks before Lisala before tonight. We can only approach Lisala by day because the obstructions are so dangerous – navigation ceases at six o'clock.

Seven p.m. Sitting in François' cabin. I am writing the day up with a glass of vino.

Climbed on top of the bridge to read this afternoon. Jean was up there laying out his salted fish to dry. A really droll, sharp-nosed dealer is Jean; he has worked the river for years, carefully weighing profit and loss as he buys and sells up and down the river. He sells anything: dope, cigarettes, tobacco, but especially fish, smoked, salted or fresh. Before he sets out, he buys things for the river people; soap goes down well – household ('coke' or 'benda') and medical ('bougaga') – and sugar, tobacco, etc. Usually he buys fish and smokes it. As you would expect with a river people there are scores of words for the different fish. He will double his pay on a journey to Kisangani.

Kalala could not be more different from Jean. He is François' *deuxième*, an intelligent, sensitive and articulate man from the Kasai, who speaks elegant French. He did three years' training to be a maths teacher, but after a year's teaching, with a wife and two young children to support (and another coming) he joined ONATRA to get a certificate in navigation – more reliable money and a chance to *faire le commerce* along the way. He wants to become a captain later, but then stop sailing and work ashore. 'I'm already making little investments. I've bought a sewing machine for my wife, so she's got a little workshop at home where she works as a seamstress.' (François brought it from Belgium: for all his bluff exterior he has a heart of gold.) Whereas Jean loves the river life, Kalala sees it another way: if the trips last two or three weeks then that's fine because it breaks the monotony of the family routine, 'which everyone who has settled down knows'; then he says he comes back feeling renewed – *'triomphant dans mon amour'* was his lovely way of putting it – vigorous and alive, wanting to live with the family again. 'If the journey lasts over a month I find it painful.'

Kalala is obviously set apart from all his shipmates. For a start, he doesn't take alcohol. His attitude to sex, for instance (he is faithful to his wife where all the others take women at every port), stems from his beliefs as a Kimbanguist, a highly moral Christian religion which looks to the Zaïrean prophet Simon Kimbangu for its doctrine. The Kimbanguists now number over six million and are recognised by the World Council of Churches, one of a number of black Christian offshoots which represent one of the most significant spiritual reactions against white colonialism in Africa. Kimbangu was imprisoned, in solitary confinement, by the Belgians (he had not preached violent revolution) and died in 1952. Kalala shows me the liturgy which he carries around with him. Apparently Kimbangu initially preached that Christ was black, though Kalala says the church now accepts that Christ was white. Why? Did Simon recant the black Jesus?

Later Kalala came down from the bridge and asked my opinion about the story of the Garden of Eden and the Fall. Is it purely symbolic? Theological discussion in midstream! I have fallen on my feet with this boat: the Belgian master with his *savoir faire* and *gastronomie*, the Kimbanguist second-in-command with his philosophical passion, the pack of thieves in the lower decks. A Conradian boat! We have stopped now (seven-thirty p.m.) where the safe channel ends. A light meal and early to bed.

Tuesday 30 March. It is about seven in the morning. Was suddenly feeling ropy last night and, sure enough, bad stomach upset and temperature this a.m. Over lunch François tells horrific stories of diarrhoea leading to death in two days – all the body's water goes! Feeling dreadful. Let's hope the Lomotil does it! Lisala port is a tiny, improvised quay beneath a steep hill. The river is all haze; it is very hot. Thankfully there is a little breeze. The far bank is almost invisible in the heat-haze; the great muddy flow of the river has all colour purged out of it by the remorseless sun. It's a hot climb up to the town, but the mission they say is cool and pleasant, and will be a change after nearly a week on the boat.

Wednesday 31 March. Well, I feel a lot better this a.m., a bit weak but the Lomotil seems – touch wood – to have done the trick. We went up to the town about three-thirty yesterday, intending to go straight to the mission. François had a packet for one of the sisters. Lisala is about the first interesting place in terms of physical geography: on a hill high above the river, with long avenues of old trees planted by the Belgians. There is a twisting road round the hill, or a stairway leading directly to the top under a canopy of trees. As you leave the river it becomes surprisingly fresh and pleasant, and you pass through wide open spaces. The first touch of European *jardin* since we were here. The locals invite us for a beer at the hotel before going to the mission, and of course we accept.

Afterwards, as dusk comes on, we walk up the track to the mission: past the Catholic *école* where the huge church can be fully seen (built around 1914). The mission is truly vast – with many enclosures and buildings behind the church and refectory-cum-dormitory-cum-administration building, built only in the fifties. Looks a bit like the New Building in the Bodleian. Here we meet Père Albert, the Flemish head of the mission. He arrives on his cherished BMW motor-bike, with a great white beard like Léopold II, T-shirt and slacks. He pulls out a packet of Rizlas and lights a hand-rolled in a cigarette-holder. He and François exchange a few words in Flemish.

We enter the ground floor of the new building. It is dim and subdued with a bare elegance about it. Tables laid for dinner. A refrigerator hums and judders in the corner. What an enormous act of faith this was: how assured they must have felt of the future – even in the late fifties (quite unaware of the imminent and sudden collapse of Belgian power) – to build such a place.

Now, he says, *la foi recule*; they have a dozen *pères* and eight *soeurs* here, but all are old (he himself has been in Zaïre since 1945) and when they are gone, and there are only black priests, it will fall. In a hundred years it could all be ruins, overgrown by tropical vegetation, returned to Africa. The young are going back to the old ways and the old beliefs: 'It is generally much worse here now than it was at independence. Nobody wants to work.' He understands why, of course, but he could never admit it. Self-delusion is necessary to those whites who still think the old ways can work.

Albert and his fellows run the mission, and the teaching, not the church itself, which has Zaïrean staff. Is he an optimist still? *'Ah, c'est une autre chose.'* Another case of *la fièvre africaine*?

The electric light flickers – electricity goes off at nine – 'You always have to take precautions and think ahead,' says Père Albert, as he decants cold water into the jugs. 'You can never be sure what will happen a few days, or even a few hours, hence.'

On the sideboard a colour picture of a white-bearded old man – the octogenarian priest from the mission we had visited at Makanza last week. Now dead. Everywhere signs of decline. The great building of the boys' school next to the church is now deserted and returning to the virgin forest. I remember Conrad's line about the Congo forest – its ominous presence, 'as if waiting for the passing of a fantastic invasion'. Sitting in the dim-lit refectory at the Lisala mission, one felt that Africa's patience would outlast the fragile bonds of faith: ultimately this mission is the white man's world.

We return in darkness through the open piazza of Lisala. Sounds of music, chatter, an accordion, melodious and mournful; fine dust as thick and soft as sand beneath our feet; occasional fires, the night flies. Down the steps – the boat is the one light on the river – and back aboard. François wants to go on the town later; I'm going to sleep off my bug. Still terribly weak – could hardly walk back. Absolutely desperate for liquid (couldn't drink the beer at the hotel – only wanted water, and they had none). I go to bed at eight-thirtyish and sleep better than I have so far on the boat.

Most of the crew have got women for the night – a dozen on the boat. The *chef ingénieur*, who is around fifty, has a girl of fifteen. Two women have paid to stay on to Kisangani.

Thursday 1 April. François, who had drunk a lot of beer (was that all?), was feeling extremely the worse for wear this a.m. First time I've seen him in such a state!

I felt a bit better this morning – managed an omelette for breakfast. It is now eight o'clock, and we are passing an enormous forest destroyed by lightning and fire – miles of stripped stumps. The river is still hazy, but early morning, five-thirty to six, was blissfully cool. Mist hung over the surface and the sun rose indistinct and yellow, water like a mirror. Should reach Bumba by nightfall.

Seven p.m. Bumba. Just arrived. A bigger dock than Lisala. Few lights, no town visible in the darkness as we approached. François ran the searchlight along the bank and hundreds of little black kids ran along the mud-flats, shrieking, calling and waving. We eat on board.

Original estimate of food consumption was wildly out, in both quantity and variety. Down to the last meat, the wine was finished the night before last. Even worse has been the lack of variety. It would have been better to have bought from the river people like everyone else!

Friday 2 April. Up sixish – no engine starting up this a.m., as they will be loading all day. Went for a walk with Kalala up main street. Like a Wild West town but for the tall palms lining the route. Shops and stores with porticoes and sidewalk-verandas, painted different colours, faded by the sun. Dust road, swept each morning. Quite

A member of the crew prepares his mirror and razor for his morning shave

cool and pleasant. Along the river the former European houses, large and elegant, columned verandas, overhanging corrugated roofs, all in the shade of palms planted in neat rows. Like a Mediterranean garden. At the bank, tied to a palm-tree, a little steamer from the colonial era, now looks as if it is just lived in. Near it is a bigger three-decker steamer, old and dirty, the rows of cabins gradually disgorging travellers (poor and black) who wash, brush their teeth, or sit on old deck-chairs, listening to transistors. This is the poorest kind of long-distance transport. Pushed by a small *pousseur*, they are heading tomorrow for Kisangani. In the big cabin under the wheel-house a Chinese man in a white T-shirt walks out and leans on the iron rail. He narrows his eyes, stretches, running his hands down his chest before scrutinising the early-morning world. Inside, a pretty black girl glances and moves away from the window. Below, a fat woman grabs her bright print dress round her and spits emphatically into the mass of hyacinths round the boat.

Monday 5 April. Breakfast around seven – a wonderful, huge pot of strong coffee and bread; no eggs, but the same marvellous pineapple I had last night with my *moambe*. The coffee gets me going.

34

The Hotel Dina! How shall I describe it? Here time stands still. The red plastic clock over the bar is always at six o'clock. Behind the bar a fridge (on for three hours a day) full only of Primus beer. Behind the bar two long shelves with lines of imported spirits – bottles spaced out – Johnnie Walker, Gordon's gin, Bols, Dão wine, Grant's whisky, vodka. And an old black-and-white pic of Mobutu. The barman is divinely insouciant, in a world of his own in his carefully ironed purple crêpe shirt. He sits there all hours, defeated by any request which is out of the ordinary (i.e. 'one beer with *two* glasses please'), which he greets with blank incomprehension and then interprets in his own peculiar way. His main pastime is rearranging his bottles with the most minuscule alterations of position, until some inner order has been satisfied. He does this by leaning on the bar for minutes on end, in a deep silence, scrutinising the spaces between the bottles. From the middle of the room the distances between them seem to diminish almost imperceptibly towards the outer ends of the shelves. A mistake? Or perhaps his way of attempting a trick with perspective, like the Greek temple-builders?

The task is endless but evidently totally satisfying. When he comes out of his trance and confronts the world, his eyes are wide and a little scared, as if he has confronted head-on some mathematical key to the nature of things which is at once meaningful but frightening. He lights a cigarette and breathes out, not daring to look back for fear of his nightmare coming back – an error in his system.

Over the bar area another ancient picture of a youthful Mobutu, touched-up black and white in a gold frame. Handwritten underneath in mock Gothic, '*Général du Corps d'Armée*'. Adorned in military decorations and the general's gold belt, the young Mobutu does not confront the camera as he does in all his photos today but, in the rigid, stiff posture cultivated by the Kinshasa photo-booths, stares off camera, younger and uncertain, not yet marked by power, corruption and sensuality. Yet destiny sits on his shoulders! Around the walls, canvases of modern, 'authentic' African art: bare-breasted black girls bearing jars to the well or *faisant le commerce*. From early morning to night the speakers play interminable Zaïrean music, catchy but repetitive with jangling guitars, almost Arab in tone. All the records are so badly scratched that they jump constantly or stick. Outside a path lined by mother-in-law's tongue, a hedge of thorns and the red-dust street with the ochre walls of a closed *magasin* opposite, blackened as if fired long ago. It looks like a thirties' cinema in a small northern town. That's Bumba for you.

Bumba to Kisangani (Stanleyville) was a slow haul. François had one engine down and it took him five days to cover the 240 miles. On the way he took the opportunity of taking more cargo, a consignment of teak from a timber camp near Mombongo, though to his annoyance the loading took the best part of a day. I swam in the river. The current was far too strong for me (it can be anything between eight and eleven knots) and pushed me back after a minute: best to walk a good way upstream and then swim down to *Nkoy* 7. Jean and the crew laughed to see this mooncalf frolicking in the river! We spent some time ashore at Basoko and Isangi; but by then my little patch of deck on *Nkoy* 7 was beginning to irk me: I was impatient to reach our goal and recorded little more in my diary until we docked there.

PART THREE: KISANGANI (STANLEYVILLE)

Sunday 11 April. We are in Kisangani – or Stanleyville. A name to conjure with in the history of the twentieth century. It was originally the site of one of Stanley's camps on his great journey down the Congo, then a great trading station for ivory, rubber, slaves and God knows what else. It was the headquarters of Léopold's dreadful private empire and the model for Kurtz's base in *Heart of Darkness*. Later it became a Belgian provincial capital, and was associated throughout the world with the terrible events of 1964–5 – the Simba rebellion, the massacre of some whites and thousands of blacks by the doped-up Simbas, the subsequent massacre of the Simbas themselves by Belgian paratroopers and Tshombe's white mercenaries – and the 1967 revolt of Tshombe's white mercenaries under Denard and Schramme.

The town has not recovered. It still bears the scars of uncertainty, of psychological unease. In spite of the pleasant, tree-lined avenues, colonnaded buildings (a little like Bulawayo in aspect), there are nevertheless many shops closed and boarded up, though *commerçants* have returned here, many of whom are Asian (*pace* Naipaul in *A Bend in the River*). The town has still an aura of suppressed hysteria. The war damage has not yet been quite swept up.

Monday 12 April. Yesterday was damp and dull all day – mid-morning big clouds banked up over the town, black and heavy. I missed the rain-storm itself, being with Solange P– who comes from an old *colon* family, and who took me round, but it dampened Palm Sunday for the street procession. There are few whites now, less than 400. At independence there had been over 5000. The town still looks numbed by the departure or death of virtually all its most hard-working and successful citizens.

Skirting the town centre you pass avenues of fine houses, the old European residential areas, with their gardens, verandas, loggias; all now overgrown, some well kept but most crumbling, decaying, lived in by the black successors, who look like mere squatters in the ruins of the whites who made this town. Marvellous mansions returning to the jungle, smoke-blackened and weathered; still and damp under the livid light before the storm, *orageux*. Creepers, palms, tall grass, overflowing what was the garden, splitting the brickwork, lying over roofs, rich, dank and fecund.

The forest waited patiently and now Africa is starting to take it back, this elegant precipitate of the European invasion. At the doors sit poor blacks in a stupor, as if worn out by the act of standing in the white man's place. They've got it now. But what can they do with it? They are equally powerless under their black Emperor. There are disintegrating roads and roofless emporia. The traffic lights, mildewed and corroded, blind-eyed, have not worked for years. Maybe there was never enough traffic to warrant their erection (maybe there was: I don't know), but they were a symbol of order. Winking away regular as clockwork in the middle of those hot, secure Stanleyville nights. The Europeans had come and made their kind of order out of the Heart of Darkness. But the forest has an ominous patience, as Conrad said, and now the invasion has almost passed. Things are on the ebb. But how will Africa find itself now? They are now slaves to another culture, mortgaged to palaces, airports and high rises they can't afford or even run, foreign cars they can't repair. If only they had been able to leave it alone: but inevitably they tried to build their independent selves in our image. We forced them to.

Tuesday 13 April. From Kisangani things get more difficult for travellers. After all, you can go by the regular boat service as far as Kisangani. From then on I didn't know how I would travel. A monthly steamer went from Ubundu, but I had missed it. I was told to go to the Catholic *procure* and ask advice of Mr Fixit: Père Claude.

Wednesday 14 April. Kisangani mission. The mission shop sells ivory and green malachite ashtrays and chessmen. The trade in elephant tusks is illegal, but elephant ivory can be exported if it has been worked, carved into an *objet d'art*, or a curio, as they are called: the bad art of modern Africa. The great art of the past has gone, except in the museums of Europe or, as here, in puerile copies.

'Sure we can get you upriver,' says Père Claude, youngish, with a sharp wit, who speaks immaculate English with a French-Canadian accent. Claude has brought North American business acumen to the running of this huge and fortress-like *procure* at what was once Stanley Falls. 'Sure, we can hire you space on a *baleinière* going upriver from Ubundu, if you can get to Ubundu that is – there is no chance in this season by road, and the train sometimes only goes once a month. We will be sending some gas oil up to the mission at Kindu: you can go up with it; you will need to buy your own gas oil, a few barrels: we can handle that order for you. You just pay us: we'll take cash, or American dollars, or we'll take American Express if you like.' With a century of survival in the Congo behind it, the church had learned to move with the times!

Friday 16 April. Met the archbishop Fataki, a Zaïrean from Haut Zaïre, as I left the *procure* through the garden. He is amused by my enthusiasm for what I have experienced so far in his country. His words should serve as a caution to all travellers. 'You want to understand the experience of Africa?' He smiled wryly and pursed his lips. 'For it to be truly worthwhile you should stay longer and get to know the country. You're making the same mistake as all those who come to Africa to study its customs, fly through on a lightning trip, gather a few ideas here and there and then whiz back to Europe and write a tremendous book. Don't think you're doing anything extraordinarily profound. What you should do is sail up the little rivers which flow into the great river, stop in the villages there, sleep in the huts, learn one of the languages, question the elderly people about their lives, the wise people, the religious men and so on: now that, that's a long-term job.'

Saturday 17 April. Claude phoned me at the Zaïre Palace Hotel at lunch-time: 'OK, we're sending our gas oil to Ubundu today, I've put yours with the same order. The train will leave this afternoon. You better get over the river as soon as you can.'

Departure from Kisangani. Sunset. We cross by pirogue: to the west golden streamers of cloud hang in the sky, the river burnished red; to the east the reflection of the light colours a mountain of clouds with a lurid glow. Kisangani has left me feeling melancholy. I don't know what I feel about Africa any more. History may be servitude, it may be freedom. Was Naipaul right to say so bitterly and contemptuously that Zaïre was a makeshift society unsupported by history? Or was the man on the *Kokolo* right, who said to me, 'We had a civilisation before you Europeans came here; the village. That is our tradition. It made us what we are, and we would be foolish to abandon it for what you have.' We colonised Africa, robbed it, tried to suppress its uniqueness of spirit; we gave it an illusory independence and left it to build itself in our image, while we still controlled its resources. And they are doing the best they can. The apparatus of the modern state may have fallen apart, but it isn't important that the state works. Africa works, the bush works, the river works. 'It is only the river which works in Zaïre' (local proverb). The bush and the river have always been self-sufficient: they are the constants in our story.

Sunday 18 April. I left Kisangani to pass the cataracts late on Saturday. Now a railway journey through the forest: single track, the lush leaves brushing the windows; sandwich and a bottle of Dào (Portuguese wine) which I crack with my trusty Swiss Army knife. Darkness comes on; we pass fine, sandy white clearings in the forest with long huts, fires outside them, and fireflies. Whenever we stop, the noises of the immense, cool forest come in a rush to our ears: crepitating with life. The moon is bright, lighting the clearings. Someone shouts that we are crossing the equator again. Thrown off the train at six. Had to get the gas oil off and onto the boat, wherever she is.

PART FOUR: THE *SARAH*

Tuesday 20 April. Ubundu. Time has passed it by. The port has sheds and overgrown railway sidings; at the quay lies a small river-steamer overshadowed by big, rusted, wheeled cranes which once ran on the tracks. The *Sarah* is upstream, moored at a grassy bank by a mud-flat with a wooden plank as a gangplank. She is a tiny, nondescript, modern fishing-boat with metal hull and bridge, and enough space on the hold covers to hang a tarpaulin and put down a bed. In the water by the *Sarah* a group of bare-breasted young women wash themselves and brush their teeth, constantly wrapping and rewrapping themselves with their print dresses (you can see little Zaïrean girls practising this as soon as they can walk). What beautiful skin they have, especially the strong curves of their backs. I recall Livingstone's shame at undressing in front of his bearers because his skin was so white.

Our captain arrives from the other side of the river and we push off. As we leave, a water-snake flashes across the surface of the river towards the bank: children rain stones on it; it carries on straight at them but eventually stops under the weight of hits.

Thursday 22 April. Sleeping on deck; chilly in the early hours, awake covered with dew.

My spirits lift as we move away from Kisangani with its Conradian memories. By now I am washing in the river, taking food and drink from it; from a dark presence it has become a benign companion, bearing us along serenely in its gentle embrace.

Saturday 24 April. Gradually it came down to simple things; the experience of the river gathered into a fine point. Fire in the cold dawn at Île Kweli, where the old men warmed their hands in a fire of the pirogue-maker's chippings: he chips away with his adze, the wood-smoke smell drifts over the *Sarah*. Île Kweli is a huge island covered by dense jungle and mysterious ruins: an enormous factory where people crushed palm-oil by hand in a wooden press (the same process had been done by machine there until the troubles of the sixties). The owner's house is so choked with jungle that I couldn't get to it. Traction-engines and mechanical parts lie abandoned; African huts are being constructed in the ruins. The watchman shows me where his new hut will be: on the footings of a European building. Even now the ruins seem inconceivably ancient, like Palmyra or Timgad. Was this what it was like in Britain after the fall of Rome?

Lowa: first we pass the trading station, where a huge metal river-boat lies sunk, its poop, bow and part of the bridge sticking above the sluggish current. It is beside a jetty in front of four large warehouses, now empty and boarded up; at the jetty a rail and turntable with a great winch and cogs: a metal caisson at the landing-stage. This was the important entrepôt of Lowa; not a soul lives here now; we are approaching the confluence of the Lowa and the Lualaba (Upper Congo), and what was for me the most memorable day on the river.

Men from Île Kweli making a pirogue. The *Sarah* is moored behind them

This is one of the most beautiful places on the journey, on a tall, wooded bluff above the confluence of the Lowa and the Lualaba. An old creek; a rotting wooden jetty; a handful of pirogues, some waterlogged; dense vegetation. Towering above the little inlet a fine cliff of sandstone hung with thickets and tall trees. Half-way up the cliff a ruined building – a sugar-cane or oil-processing factory, roofless, its graceful arches adding an Arcadian touch to Africa. Up the opposite side of the cliff to the ruin a stairway has been cut into the red stone, once laid with bricks, now worn away by age. At the top, *la butte*: a white house stands in a wonderful spot over the confluence, the river stretching into the blue beyond, the forest green and featureless to the horizon. A golden afternoon sun. I can make out the warehouses and the sunken boat below and away downriver. I walk along the cliff edge on an overgrown path to where a bamboo gazebo stands, placed to enjoy just that view. Now no one comes here, and the white house is empty. It is used for odd visitors to the village, says my informant. Polished stone floor, arched main room, a little terrace with a brick balustrade, tall ceilings and hardwood doors, high, shuttered windows, cool, quiet, empty; a fine yellow and gold frangipani, 15 feet high. I am momentarily struck dumb by the beauty and the inevitability of it all. Along the cliff edge to another gazebo above a vertiginous, green drop; the cleared earth of the path overgrowing again; dragonflies sun themselves. Ahead a little avenue of European houses with gardens, bushes and rows of well-established trees.

Half-an-hour walk to what was the mission. Most of the village are walking with us. We pass the school, a great thirties' building. Poor houses. The mission itself was once massive, but the *pères* and *soeurs* left in 1965 and never came back. Now there is a *pasteur*, a kind of lay minister. He had received a message from Kisangani that I might be staying. They have been so looking forward to my stay. How can I tell them that I must press on before sunset? They will be so disappointed. We go through the church to the cloister: the garden is overgrown; the buildings themselves ruinous, plaster of the ceilings falling, revealing great patches of decaying wattle. In the corridor a marvellous old coffee-grinding machine from Rochdale of all places. Into a cool, high-ceilinged room: we sit on benches round a long wooden table. The old men ask about my journey and what I am doing; their handshakes are strong and firm, their eyes full of friendship and interest. The *pasteur*'s wife has prepared a meal of cakes made out of banana and manioc, of cold curried chicken pieces, a chopped pineapple and fresh water. I told the story of the journey, and something of my life in England.

I returned to the boat, and it was there that the Christians of Lowa gave me gifts for my journey, a big enamel bowl full of rice, some eggs, and a woven basket containing three live chickens. They blessed my journey. I had nothing of any value to give in return, even had they expected it, which, the *pasteur* assured me, they did not. 'They can't afford to do this, can they?' I asked. 'No,' he replied, 'but you must accept.'

With the *pasteur*'s help I thanked them in Swahili; as we pulled away the whole village seemed to be down at the jetty waving. The afternoon sun, slanting down over the bluffs, touched the scene with gold.

This far, after the unremitting bush, I was unprepared for the magnificence of the forest, a great reef of tall hardwoods, creepers, giant palms sometimes towering 200 feet above the river, crowning ancient striated sandstone cliffs. Sometimes the

A woman outside the ruined factory at Lowa: the spirit of Africa

Villagers wave to the *Sarah* as she sails towards Kindu

roots of the big trees arch right out into the water, twisted spreads of roots, ridged cones of roots, bleached bones of roots. A pirogue weighed down to the gunwales with a family and all their earthly belongings (pushing upstream against the current) sails underneath the arches of a great tree as they make their slow passage upriver (to a new home?). The villagers all wave to us from their raffia huts; the children run along the bank screaming at us, sometimes plunge in and try to swim out, laughing. We are a spectacle!

Towards sunset bluebirds play around the boat, tirelessly swooping and soaring; occasionally a water-serpent darts across our path. The tsetse flies which cluster under the tarpaulin in the heat of the day have all gone. The chickens squawk. We have avocados and pawpaw, and better still, as the light fades, fresh water from a cold spring pouring out of the sandstone cliff like a fountain. We drink the pure, cold liquid like men in a desert. Everything comes to those who wait! Africa is working its magic.

Monday 26 April. Kindu. Journey's end. A fiendishly hot afternoon. We tie up against an old river-steamer now used as a pontoon. Unload the gear. Say goodbye. All the surplus I give to the crew of the *Sarah*: I hadn't the heart to eat the chickens and gave them to the boys. The mission jeep meets us, to take us up to the town. First impressions: the Arab and Indian world is here. In the days of Livingstone and Stanley this was about as far as the Arab entrepreneurs, slavers like Tippu Tib, had penetrated westwards down the Luava to the Congo at Nyangwe. The shops have verandas and wooden fronts, the names are Patel, Kikim Pop and Sharma Dasharath; the swastika is emblazoned on a clothing shop; old Muslim men with white caps sit under the verandas on the main street, operating old Singer sewing-machines. In the shops: Hindu calendars printed in Nairobi, Necko medical soap from Bombay, Chinese razors in their little coloured cardboard boxes with flip-up mirrors; the stock is that of the fifties' corner shop: little tins of Vick, small packets of Omo and Carnation milk. These are Naipaul's traders, pushing eastwards when driven out of Uganda or wherever; always willing and able to start anew. They all have Mobutu's picture prominently displayed.

The hotel: Le Relais. The last stop. My host built the hotel in 1952; the main bar doubles for the cinema in Kindu; the Wurlitzer has records in Spanish, Portuguese, French, Flemish and English; he has made a lovely garden. 'I'm going back to Europe next year,' he says. 'I cannot fight any more.'

My room is clean. There is a green mantis in the bathroom and french windows open onto the lovely garden with kept grass, mature trees and frangipani.

Tuesday 27 April. I feel sad to be going back. I have the map open on the bed: from Kindu it is possible to take a train south for 200–300 miles to Kabalo where another long navigable stretch of the river begins: it used to be possible to take smaller boats through the marshy region around Lake Upemba for about 300 miles more down to Bukama, there to pick up the train to Likasi and Lubumbashi. It is there, in the highlands of Shaba-Katanga, that the Lualaba rises, in that great watershed which divides Angola, Zaïre and Zambia, where the Zambezi also rises, to flow southwards. But no one knows whether the train runs; some say there is no boat service any more through the papyrus-choked marshes of the upper Lualaba. In any case such thoughts are pointless: I have run out of time. At least, this time.

There is no harbour, not even a quay, at Kindu. On one of the two or three disused old metal-bodied river-boats used as pontoons, inside the locked wheel-house three decks up, the captain's telescope, maps and instruments lie on the table. The bank is covered with thick, long grass, bushes and palms. At the arrival of any boat, children come down from the huts up the slope and stare. The boat back to Ubundu is called the *Luama*, a wood-burning stern-wheeler built in Belgium forty or fifty years ago. She is run by a little private boat company, has two flimsy decks, and a spindly funnel, a bowsprit and a little crane for lifting the bundles of wood and papyrus leaves which she uses for fuel. She makes about five knots against the current, and has to stop each day for wood, as she goes up and down between Ubundu and Kindu. She has an open bridge with a big wheel, canvas drapes along the rails in front of the cabins to protect passengers from the heat; children shriek and splash in the water

A stern-wheel paddle-boat, the *Luama*

overflowing from leaky pipes. There is no other way except the river: there still is no good road. The captain, Citoyen Ntumba wa Kala, is a gentle man, and to him I told the tale of my journey.

In a sense the journey still goes on. The *Luama* still plies her monthly trade, wheezing and creaking between Ubundu and Kindu. And my journey too still continues in the mind's eye; as the ambassador and the archbishop said it would. It would indeed need a longer voyage, and a slower one, truly to comprehend what I saw, and the spirit of the people who gave me their friendship. That (dare I say it?) is the spirit of Africa. Once you have experienced it with an open heart, you never forget it.

THE SEPIK
AND THE WAGHI
Christina Dodwell

When every mountain in the Alps has been scaled, and even the Himalayas made the scene of mountaineering triumphs; when shooting buffaloes in the Rockies is almost as common as potting grouse on the moors . . . it comes with a sense of relief to visit a country really new, about which little is known.

Reverend Samuel McFarlane, *Among the Cannibals of New Guinea*

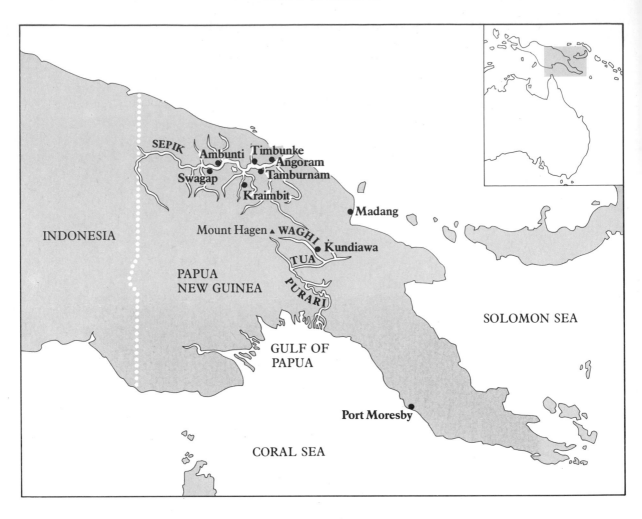

Shaped like a dead turkey, New Guinea lies just south of the equator, between Indonesia and Australia. It is the second-largest island in the world. Broken mountain ranges, torrential rivers and thick jungle make it a difficult place to visit. Only one road leads from the coast into the highland interior, and there are large tracts of little-explored territory containing some tribes which are just emerging from the Stone Age. The land's ruggedness has divided its peoples into distinctly separate groups; it is estimated to hold 1000 different tribes.

There are stocky, dark-skinned highlanders, warrior farmers, coal-black, 6-foot-tall men, peaceful islanders, hook-nosed swamp-dwellers, Melanesians, Micronesians and Polynesians; there are men who wear pigs' tusks through their noses, feathers in their hair, ornate flower-decked wigs; for clothes some wear leaves, loincloths or phallic gourds. Myths, magic, initiation rites, witch-doctors, head-hunters; there are men who used to puncture their enemies' skulls and suck out the brains, people who smoke-preserved their dead relatives, and others who ate the dead as an act of love. In the accessible areas of Papua New Guinea many of these primitive customs have died out, but in parts of the country's interior some ancient ways are still practised. A few of these strange customs I was both to see and experience personally during my visit.

My journey would be an attempt to travel across the country by river, going up the Sepik River in the north then southwards down the Waghi, a river which had never been navigated and which runs through one of the least-explored parts of Papua New Guinea. In contrast to the Sepik's placid river-current, the Waghi is a white-water river, having many rapids. It is among the wildest whitewater rivers in the Pacific, and is locally known as 'The Eater of Men'. To attempt this descent of the Waghi I would join up with a team of American river-rafters. I had accepted their invitation with slight nervousness, never having tried whitewater rafting, but it sounded like an exciting way to learn.

This would not be my first visit to Papua New Guinea. In 1980–1 I had travelled extensively in remote areas, on horseback and on foot, and by paddling a dugout canoe. One of the journeys took twelve weeks of paddling on the Sepik River and its tributaries. It had been a colourful, memorable trip, and was the first time that a westerner, let alone a woman, had paddled the Sepik River. But this time I would be going up the river by boat.

I came into Madang harbour, a big port near the Sepik, on the SS *Umboi*, passing through a seeming maze of palm-fringed coral islands set in a turquoise sea. When the ship docked at a small wharf, I picked up my brown holdall and disembarked along with fifty local people who carried baskets, suitcases, babies and branches of bananas. Few passengers used the gangway; most just clambered off the ship on to the narrow wharf which was already crowded with cargo stacked in boxes and with mounds of old car tyres. In the noise of engines and voices I heard someone say crossly, '*Kum huri-up. Yu-mi no kan waistim taim; wokabaut strong, ta'sol.*' To understand the words they must be read aloud. This is Pidgin, the language which has emerged because Papua New Guinea's 1000 tribes speak over 700 different languages.

After making enquiries about Sepik boats I discovered that most vessels ferry cargo and passengers to the offshore islands, not to the Sepik, and when I asked if the government boat was planning a patrol, a man replied, '*Bot i no-gud, i dai finis.*' In fact it had wood-rot and was no longer safe.

The search for a boat took me to small wharves and slipways all around the town peninsula, which has great charm and an old colonial atmosphere, reflected by places like the Smugglers' Inn, the Royal Yacht Club, and the Madang Country Club where I stopped to watch men playing outdoor bowls. The men wore white attire and floppy-brimmed hats. It is surprising to think that in 1883, a hundred years ago, there were only five resident Europeans in the whole of Papua New Guinea.

Colonisation came late, mostly within this century, hampered by the obstacles of harsh terrain, climate, fever and unfriendly natives. Since that time, the development of copper, gold, copra and coffee has catapulted the country from the Stone Age into modern times. Independent since 1975, the Government is rightly admired for its non-corrupt, steady and reasonable attitudes. When I met the Prime Minister, Michael Somare, at his house, he told me that he believes in slow, grass-roots development, building from the ground and not hurrying. Then he added, 'Some people think that the Sepik is the end of the world, but for those who live there, it's only the beginning.'

After seeing more boats I made arrangements to travel all the way to the Upper Sepik in a missionary boat called the *Kaseli*. Built in 1942, the *Kaseli* was 45 feet long and made of wood with multicoloured paintwork; it had a funnel and small, airy decks, well scrubbed and clean. Its cargo for the first stage of the journey was a piano.

The voyage began on time and the *Kaseli* chugged north-west along the coast, from a shore-line of coconut plantations to one of malarial mangrove swamps backed by equatorial jungle. The mouth of the Sepik is marked by a muddy stain, miles wide, where its waters meet the blue ocean. The Sepik's annual water-flow makes it one of the world's largest rivers; it is 750 miles long, and is navigable by steamer for about 300 miles; parts of the Sepik River are well known and accessible to tourists, while missionaries and miners use it instead of a road.

The *Kaseli*'s first stop was at the Lower Sepik town of Angoram, where it was to deliver the piano to a mission and to collect some oil-drums. '*Tro-im-awai anka*' (drop the anchor), shouted the captain as the boat was made secure for the night.

Early in the morning, while waiting for the *Kaseli* to depart, I made a quick trip to the market-place to get some supplies of pineapples, papaya, sugar-cane and smoked fish. A woman selling smoked nail-fish and *makau* (tilapia) looked at me in amazement and said, 'Christina?' It was Jane, a young woman from the Blackwater tributary where I had spent a month during my canoe-journey. I was delighted to find an acquaintance but I wasn't surprised at her remembering me. What had been surprising was the number of people, including nationals and expatriates in cities and villages, who, since my return to Papua New Guinea, had recognised and called me by name. The nationals didn't shout the name loudly or demand attention, they just called it softly within my hearing, and smiled with delight when I greeted them in their language.

Jane's mother, an old, wrinkled lady with grey, poppled hair, had also come downriver to market. Both women clasped my hands, telling me the news of their village, and they gave me several smoked fish wrapped in banana leaves.

After leaving Angoram the river was peaceful, the only traffic some motor-canoes laden with cargo and passengers who held brightly-coloured umbrellas to give shade from the hot sun. Along the river-banks I noticed some bush fires, their pale smoke spiralling up into the sky. As we went past the fires their ash rained down in the air, and as the smoke billowed above us it veiled the sun, giving the light an odd, pink glow. The *Kaseli*'s captain, Joseph, a barrel-chested man with weather-beaten face, told me that the lighting of these fires is usually deliberate. It was now the dry season and the river-level was low enough for villages to clear fertile riverside plots and cultivate some vegetables before the yearly flood-waters return.

Lying in a broad, swampy valley, the lower river is about half a mile wide, and its course meanders through the forest in huge, sweeping bends like a giant, flat snake. I leaned against the *Kaseli*'s prow-rails, feeling contented. There was only one other passenger, a local pastor, slim and frizzy-haired, with a benign expression. His name was Pastor Peter, a western name because as a Christian he was given a Christian name. He told me that the boat's name, *Kaseli*, means 'light' and its work is to transport cargo and mission workers, and to make district visits.

In the late afternoon we reached Tamburnam village. Captain Joseph manoeuvred the *Kaseli* as close as he dared to their shallow river-front, and because there was no depth-testing equipment the crew tested the water's depth by using a metal weight tied onto a rope. They kept encouraging the captain forward but he was grumbling that he'd be blamed if the *Kaseli* ran aground (*ol bai kilim mi sapos* Kaseli *i stap bugarup*).

The village consisted of big family huts raised on stilts 10 feet off the ground, protecting the occupants from the annual floods. When I went ashore, I was taken to greet the headman and a *bigman* (village elder) called Anton, whose three wives had looked after me during my last visit. I was looking forward to seeing them again and I had brought gifts of cloth sarongs for them, though it turned out that one wife had gone. Anton said he had sent her back to her family because she was too bad-tempered. The remaining two wives were raggedly dressed but cheerful women, and their twelve offspring looked well fed and healthy.

Villagers on the bank of the Upper Sepik still rely on bows and arrows to hunt for their food

To Anton I gave a wood-carving knife because most Sepik men are talented sculptors of wood. It is a traditional art, and the men create statues, masks, ancestor faces, animals and spirit figures; the carvings are usually large, primitive and phallic. Anton strolled with me through the village and we often paused to look at the carvings stored in the open workshops between the stilts that supported the houses. Sepik art has been known to collectors since about 1920, and nowadays the sale of carvings to passing tourists is a thriving business, bringing a steady and much-wanted flow of cash into their subsistence economy. A good carving fetches a high price because the only tourists who can afford to visit the Sepik are wealthy ones (or those with unlimited time).

We watched a boy tending some baby crocodiles in a fenced enclosure on the bank. He gave them fresh water and then grabbed one of them by its neck and tail; it hissed angrily at us. Anton said that crocodiles are plentiful in the Sepik, and young ones which get caught in fish-traps are kept until they are large enough to slaughter for their skin.

At sunset some women took me to have a bath in the river. They assured me that crocodiles are timid and do not stay around the villages. We wore sarongs; the water was warm and muddy. Dugout canoes with carved crocodile-head prows scurried to and fro across the river; they were long, narrow canoes, paddled by women returning from their vegetable gardens, or bringing in their catch of fish and prawns, collected in large bottle-neck baskets: they made dramatic silhouettes against the setting red sun. I returned to the *Kaseli* to sleep, rigging my hammock and mosquito net at the stern and settling down for a peaceful night. Mosquitoes can be atrocious in the rainy season, but it was now the dry season and there were fewer.

The *Kaseli* didn't make a dawn start the next morning, and from my hammock I watched the village coming to life, through the mist which hung over the glassy river. Noises of firewood being chopped, cocks crowing, dogs quarrelling, mixed with women's shrill voices calling to each other as they paddled away to find fish. Other women were at work pounding sago, beating the fibrous pith in the trunks of sago palms, then washing it and straining the residue to make sago flour, the staple diet of the Sepik.

Regular thuds in different rhythms sounded as men on the shore began to hew out the centre of a hardwood tree, in order to make a new canoe. I went ashore to watch a finished one being 'cooked'; the men set fire to bundles of dry palm branches, then fanned the flames against the canoe to shrink and seal its exterior. They gave extra care to the grisly-jawed crocodile head at its prow. It is the custom to carve a crocodile's head at the prow because according to Sepik folklore the world was created by crocodiles, and original man was born from a crocodile. No woman was born, the man was all alone; his sorrow was so great that he wept and his tears became the Sepik River. The crocodile is not a loving god, he is more like the Devil, ruling by fear and preying on superstition.

We left Tamburnam, and work began aboard the *Kaseli* as its crew sluiced down the decks and swabbed them with mops and brooms. I retreated to the back roof and sat on top of it, sipping coffee, eating papaya, and watching the flow of the river.

A speedboat containing a Catholic priest passed the *Kaseli*, and it wasn't long

After a canoe has been hollowed out of a log by axe, it is then 'cooked' by fire to shrink and seal it

before Timbunke came into sight. The *Kaseli* went alongside the river-bank, dropped anchor and for extra security the crew tied the mooring-ropes around a tree on the shore. Timbunke is a village with a flourishing Catholic mission and two white fathers came down to greet me. One was the visiting father who'd overtaken the *Kaseli* and the other was an Irishman, Father Mike O'Donovan, who showed me around the mission station, talking animatedly about his work and beliefs. Outside the church some men were carving a life-size wooden statue of St Paul to commemorate the Catholics' fiftieth year in Timbunke. Father Mike explained the importance of using a local tree and carving it in the traditional way, rather than having an imported, western-style statue. 'People should not think that imported things are better,' he said, 'we want the church to belong to the people in the traditional way, a Sepik interpretation of the Bible.'

Above the church altar was a carving of a Sepik man being crucified, and the church-bell was a wooden log-drum. Apart from church work the mission runs a community school, a small hospital, and a nursing school for aid-post orderlies; it also manages outlying aid posts and sends clinics and vaccine patrols by boat into isolated areas.

Father Mike continued our tour by taking me across a log-bridge over a picturesque creek and through Timbunke village, which has the oldest *haus tamboran* (spirit house) on the Sepik. Many, not all, villages have a *haus tamboran*, which is home to all the ancestor spirits and to nature spirits of animist origin. The *haus* is used for tribal ceremonies, but it is also a meeting-place for the elders, a council chamber at times of village decisions, and a repository for sacred carvings. By tradition no women are allowed in these houses, but due to tourism it is a source of income and so the headman relaxes this rule for foreigners.

The cool shade was a welcome relief and as my eyes adjusted to the gloom I saw seven *garamuts* (big log-drums made from 8-foot lengths of tree-trunk), which Father Mike said had been hollowed out through a narrow slit by stone-adze. Then he directed my attention to a tall, three-legged Sepik chair with a carved wooden man sitting on it, which he called the 'seat of wisdom'. 'The figure is called Kisameri,' he told me in his lilting Irish accent. 'It means that he's a very wise man and when people want to make serious decisions, they consult him by touching the carving. It's like a prophet of old, if you can compare the two, like Moses, for example. And Kisameri I think has a lot in common with him.'

I had been wondering about the effect of the mission on the village, and was impressed by the way it seemed to offer an improved quality of life without wiping out all the traditional ways and beliefs. But sometimes, it seems, God is simply added onto the line of dead ancestors and nature spirits. However, traditional life is based on the joint activity of all spiritual forces, and people's well-being depends on recognising and paying respect to each of these forces.

After reboarding the *Kaseli* and waving goodbye to Timbunke, I joined the crew for a snack of smoked fish and *parem* (sago bread), then found a cool, quiet place where I could dangle my feet in the river as we chugged slowly along. I watched a fisherman in a canoe stopping to drink from the river; he drank by flicking handfuls of water upwards into the air and catching some of it in his mouth.

Pastor Peter came over and asked me why I travel, so I tried to explain it by saying that missionaries follow the call of God, while I follow the call of wild places. Often my travels are simply caused by my curiosity to see what is around the next corner or over the next hill, to learn what lies beyond the horizons.

It was a hot afternoon. I pulled a bucket of water on a rope up to the back deck and washed my clothes. I was finishing hanging them to dry over the back rails when I heard someone calling out to the *Kaseli* from a motor-canoe. It was a sun-tanned Australian old-timer accompanied by a local woman and half a dozen smiling, coffee-coloured children; the man kept shouting and gesturing to a cloth bag in his hand so we beckoned their canoe over to the *Kaseli* and invited them aboard to show us what was in the bag.

It held crocodile teeth carved with Sepik designs, and while I admired them the man introduced himself as Jeff Liversedge and said he lived on the river-bank with his wife and family. 'I always try selling teeth to tourists, they like to buy them,' he said, and indeed they were lovely but expensive. He went on to tell me that crocodiles are not an endangered species in the Sepik. Each adult female lays fifty to eighty eggs a year, and everyone is allowed to hunt them. Jeff had been hunting them professionally for twenty years. He added that he planned to hunt crocodiles that evening and he invited me to go with him. The sun was going down and since the *Kaseli* didn't run at night I knew it couldn't leave me behind, so I clambered down into Jeff's canoe. Before setting out we took Jeff's family to their home and Jeff told me the story of how he met his wife in a nearby village and ran away with her. The couple hid out in the swamps for a week before they dared to return and set up house.

At the ramshackle house we collected two men with axes, and a spear, then went speeding off in the motor-canoe towards a creek. I asked if it wasn't easier to hunt crocodiles at night by spotlight and Jeff replied that when crocodiles are around, any time is good for hunting them. The men's eyes followed the shore-line of *pitpit* grass and mud-banks, checking for any signs of slide-marks. Jeff commented that we weren't looking for a large one as it is illegal to kill oversize crocodiles; the best size for skin-trading is 4 to 6 feet in length.

After a long time the man at the canoe's nose pointed to a slide-mark left by a fair-sized crocodile; he seized the spear and stood still and alert for an instant before hurling it at a target that I couldn't see. The thrashing of water proved his skill and he pulled in his catch, a 5-foot crocodile which was quickly killed by axe. Being squeamish about blood, I couldn't bear to watch the killing, but the skinning was so interesting that I forgot about my distress. Thick, white sinews attached the skin to the body, and its head had the several extra breathing-valves which enable a crocodile to swim underwater while gripping its victim, without flooding its breathing system. Some steaks of tail-meat were given to me and I later cooked them aboard the *Kaseli* for supper. It was fishy-tasting white meat, rather like lobster.

The *Kaseli*'s engines were started at dawn and soon we were cruising upriver, hoping to reach the government outstation of Ambunti, 70 miles away, before night-fall. In the river-current there was a lot of salvinia, the surface-weed that has plagued the Sepik for the past ten years. With trailing roots it forms mats that cause problems for canoes and fishing. River traffic was scarce although we passed some floating, grassy islands as big as boats, which were surrounded by clusters of paddle-canoes as the villagers picked the tasty spinach that grows among the grasses. Other small canoes, some propelled by five-year-old children who stood up fearlessly to paddle, were going about their daily business on the river. They disturbed two cockatoos which whirred into flight, screeching noisily and flying in erratic bursts, soaring and diving. Bird-life in the Sepik is fairly colourful; there are over 600 species of birds in Papua New Guinea, including thirty-six different types of birds of paradise whose spectacular and colourful plumage gives them the reputation of being the most beautiful birds in existence.

As we progressed upriver, I took a turn at steering the *Kaseli* with the ship's wheel, then went to find my map. The moment I spread it out on the front deck, Captain Joseph and three crew members sat down beside me and started trying to guess the *Kaseli*'s position. They didn't have any maps, but navigated by experience, and were intrigued to see the plan of the river laid out before them. The captain was so fascinated that I gave the map to him as a present.

All afternoon the sun glared down on the river but as we approached Ambunti the sky went dark and rain poured down over the *Kaseli*. It was an equatorial rain-storm

Above: the Sepik River at dusk. Right: the *Kaseli* passes one of the villages which cluster along the banks of the Sepik River

and I was glad to be under shelter, but the crew didn't seem to mind the downpour; they grabbed some mops and brooms, then went outside to wash the roofs and funnel.

The *Kaseli* reached Ambunti several hours after dark, using a spotlight and the captain's instinct to find the way. The crew were keen to get there because the following day was Saturday, their Sabbath, a day of rest or holiday.

That next morning I watched Papua New Guinea's national flag being raised outside Ambunti government office, and met the district *kiap* (officer in charge), John Saia, beside a remarkable building without walls which he said was the Ambunti court-house. Its thatched roof was lined inside with paintings, coloured mud designs on canvases of woody *limbum*, and its rafters and pillars were richly carved with primitive phallic images. The *kiap* told me that he is also the magistrate and when I asked what sort of cases are heard in this court-house he told me about recent cases of assault, spreading false reports, and use of malicious magic or sorcery. A few months ago a man had pleaded guilty to a charge of intent to harm by sorcery; the victim had died while out fishing in his canoe.

Guilty people are usually sentenced to several months in the local prison, which only had a small wire fence around it. I asked if there were many escapees and the *kiap* replied that no one bothers to run away. 'Then why are they building a second fence?' I said, gesturing to the rows of big, new wooden posts. 'Oh, that's because the prisoners get too many visitors; the new fence is to keep people out.'

54

In general it is simple to keep law and order, explained John, except in villages where the elders don't agree with a law. It is hard for old men, empowered by generations of traditional clan-law, to give way to clean-shaven youths from different tribes, representing an authority called Government. Although the Government consists of Papua New Guinean nationals, the individual tribes tend to treat each other with suspicion, and *kiaps* are not given jobs near their homes lest they be corrupted by pressure from their family lines and tribal elders.

Upriver from Ambunti is a village, Swagap, which has long aggravated the authorities by refusing to accept the Government; they used to attack official patrols and fired with bows and arrows at anyone who ventured too near. They have become quieter over the years but still have a bad reputation; even when they took me as a guest to their village in 1980 they had treated me with surly distrust. I had decided to make a short detour and visit them again and I wondered how they would react to seeing me this time.

A Swagap warrior shows off his spears, used against humans as well as animals.
Several years ago Swagap warriors killed government officers who came to the village.
They hate any outsiders

The *Kaseli* cruised slowly upriver; now that we had reached the Upper Sepik the river was getting narrower and smaller, and the terrain was growing wilder with mountainous banks covered in jungle growth. Great garamut trees with flange-buttressed roots, ginger plants, pepper trees, stilt-rooted pandanus pines draped with vines, all created a kaleidoscope of green, with here and there splashes of vivid scarlet from D'Albertis creepers.

Swagap is located several miles up a tributary stream but Captain Joseph lent me the *Kaseli*'s motor-dinghy to get there. Swagap's sinister atmosphere had not changed; perhaps it was due to the four *haus tamborans* (there is usually just one) in the village, although the people were more cordial than before. They had just finished burning down the oldest of their *haus tamborans* because it had served for the correct number of years, and outside it were many baskets of sago, smoked wild pig and smoked crocodile. Village men wearing loincloths and shell decorations stood around in groups and since most of them carried bows and arrows I asked them to demonstrate their skill as archers. They obligingly agreed, and the performance turned into quite a competition with twenty men firing arrows at a wooden target. Then they showed me the different types of bamboo arrows and wooden spears they use for killing men, wild animals, birds and fish, and they boasted of the men they had killed. About ten years ago they had shot some government employees they had discovered on a patrol boat in their stream.

There was one other special village that I wanted to revisit, Kraimbit, where I had stayed for a month in 1980. Kraimbit lies far up the Blackwater tributary river so I borrowed a motor-canoe for two days. The journey to Kraimbit wasn't easy because, this being the dry season, the water-level was 15 to 20 feet lower than on my previous visit, and what had formerly been a maze of lakes and rivers was now a vast mud-flat with a few streams. The canoe kept running aground and the boatman said he was lost. Finally I got out to see if I could find out where we were, but after a short distance I walked into deep mud, suddenly sinking to my hips in wet ooze which cloyed around my legs. I had to struggle quite hard to get back onto firm ground. After floundering out, hot, wet and mud-covered, I went and lay in the stream to wash the mud off before rejoining the boatman. But I refused to feel ruffled, telling myself that one must not expect things to be easy; after all, this is New Guinea. And I was looking forward to reaching Kraimbit again, having kept in touch with people there over several years by letter (airmail/canoemail). Finally some children in a paddle-canoe came along and, promising to send help back to the boatman, I took a lift with the children to Kraimbit.

When the Kraimbits saw me arrive they began calling to each other in excitement and many came running through the village. It was a wonderful welcome; I shook hands with everyone and couldn't stop smiling while their eyes shone and their faces beamed with pleasure. Some *bigmen* and the headman, Kansol Otto, hurried over to welcome me. They took me to a shade-shelter, brought fruit for refreshment, and we all sat down together to exchange news.

One major event for them had been the construction of a new *haus tamboran*, a magnificent, large house on carved stilts which dominated the centre of the village. Traditional, spiritual beliefs are rigorously followed here; Kansol Otto had not

Women of Kraimbit. Left: weaving baskets. Right: the shells are part of the payment for the bride by her husband

allowed me to use the men's path, but had brought me on the women's path, and I wondered if I would be admitted into this new *haus tamboran*. I had been the only woman to go into their last one; at the time they had said that because of the way I had come to visit them – alone, by canoe – they would give me the freedom of the *haus tamboran* and treat me as an honorary man.

So I asked Otto if the committee of the *haus tamboran* would let me inside this new one. Otto's face clouded over and he fumbled for words. The hesitation surprised me, but soon I realised that it came from their fear of the *tamboran* and its power; they didn't want to put me in danger.

After a meeting of elders it was decided that I should be reinitiated into the new *haus tamboran*, along with some other initiates. I was guided to a line of solemn men which I joined and we walked along the men's path and up the bamboo ladder into the *haus*. In the shady half-light I presented gifts to the committee, Otto and various *bigmen*, under the eye of the *tamboran*. Five old men began playing their sacred bamboo 'flutes'; holding the long, fat bamboo tubes out sideways, they danced in circles, all keeping the same complex foot-rhythm, and blowing through the bamboo to produce mellow, braying harmonies. Some bamboo flutes were decorated with canework and feathers, some can only be played by one man and are thought to have the power to produce only one specific song.

Otto brought my attention to a group of boys and young men, and said that they were now ready for their initiation into manhood through the skin-cutting ordeal.

58

This is a blood ritual dedicated to crocodiles, a rare and dramatic ceremony at which the initiates' bodies are cut and sliced to represent their battle with the Devil crocodile, and their rebirth as crocodile-men.

If I look at this from a westerner's viewpoint it seems a barbaric and savage ritual, but from the Kraimbits' perspective it is the customary mark of manhood and they bear the scars with pride. The initiates explained to me that by going voluntarily through the pain and fear of the ceremony they would emerge as men, wearing the scars as an outward sign of their courage and fortitude, and as a reminder that they should never again be afraid. One initiate, Rassell, was only twelve years old and he was clearly terrified of the whole idea, but he said that he was ready to face it. Many of the men sitting around me had the scars of skin-cutting; raised series of bumps from their backs over their shoulders and down to their stomachs, with crocodile eyes cut on their chests.

Everything was ready, people were in a festive mood, and after a while the committee announced that the initiation would start that evening.

In the late afternoon the villagers went to decorate themselves, painting coloured mud ochres on their bodies and shaking out their head-dresses of fur and feathers. I went to wash at a small, cool spring in the sago-palm forest, using a coconut-shell to scoop up the water and pour it over myself. Then I hurried back to watch the menfolk, now in full *bilas* (body decoration), marching through the village and into the *haus tamboran*. Soon the throbbing of drums began to resound from the *haus*.

The women were chanting and dancing around outside the *haus*, dancing with small steps and flicking their hips to swing their grass skirts. At dusk the initiates were brought outside like prisoners with their hands held above their heads and grasses in their mouths. Suddenly the women surged forward and pretended to try to wrestle their sons from the men's grasp, but after a scuffle they were beaten into retreat, and the boys went back inside the *haus*. Papa Lucas (my proxy father in Kraimbit) took me with them up the ladder into the *haus*, into a scene of drumming and dancing as men stomped in rings, jangling their shell leg-bands and chanting in rising waves of oh-ee-ay.

As more men gradually joined in the dance they formed wheels within wheels, each going at a different speed. They kept it up all night, while the women held a different kind of *singsing* in a big family house nearby. Long after dark when I left the *haus tamboran* and went to the women's house, I found the women sitting cross-legged on the floor around some kerosene lanterns, mothering their babies and chanting a chorus, while in the centre of the hut three women stood singing solos, calling to their sons (the initiates) not to be afraid of the crocodile's bite. Other women stood to lead different chants; Papa Lucas' wife led a chant of happiness at my return and everyone in the house stood up to join in.

In the deep of the night I went back to the *haus tamboran* to watch as the wheeling circle of men generated the power of the *tamboran*. Initiation includes the boys' entry into the secrets of their ancestors and nature spirits, things beyond the comprehensible, whose powers are called up during the night in rituals which are taboo to outsiders; it would not be proper to describe them here.

At dawn the three initiates were taken by a silent crocodile-line of men to wash in the creek, and when they came back they sat on *limbum* mats outside the *haus tamboran*, ready for the skin-cutting to begin.

The first cuts of the razor blades on the boys' chests drew half-circles around their nipples, four half-circles over a quarter-inch deep. Blood ran from the slashes and, feeling dizzy, I sat down hurriedly. Two initiates beside me were gritting their teeth against the pain, but the third, young Rassell, was screaming loudly with terror. I felt sorry for him but his companions told him sternly, 'We must bleed, to let out our mother's blood so we become men.'

His screams did not stop and after making the minimum markings the *haus tamboran*'s committee let him go, which was a relief since no one intended the boy to suffer overmuch. Meanwhile, on the other two boys' shoulders and backs the skin-cutters were making a wide series of slashes like scale-markings, and helpers used wodges of grass to mop away the flows of blood.

About an hour later when their skin-cutting was over, the boys' cuts were anointed with plant oil and red mud (which effectively prevents infections).

Then it was my turn. I wanted to complete my initiation into the new *haus tamboran*, feeling that I was no longer an outsider to the Sepik customs or to the people who had adopted me, and so I let the villagers mark me with the crocodile's bite on my left shoulder. It was painful, and as the razor blade kept ripping through my skin, I winced and clenched my hands. Papa Lucas told me I must be brave in order to emerge strong, like a crocodile, never to be afraid again.

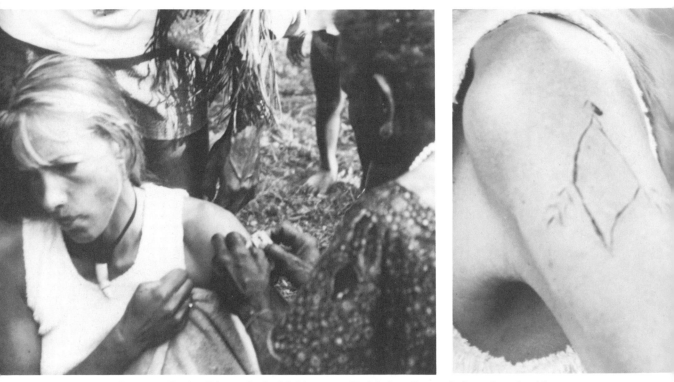

Christina Dodwell is marked with 'the crocodile bite', a diamond-shaped mark with decorative fletchings

The missionary pastor travelling on the *Kaseli* stops to baptise new converts in the Sepik River

A village headman shows Christina Dodwell what he is having for dinner – smoked wild pig and crocodile meat

Christina Dodwell looks on as an initiate from Kraimbit has his skin cut with crocodile scale markings, to show he has entered manhood

A tribesman wearing traditional paint and feathers for the *singsing* which launched the rafting trip

Christina Dodwell and crew poised to enter a rafter's nightmare – a turbulent 'hole' which could suck a boat and crew underwater and keep it there indefinitely

Expedition leader, Skip Horner, with Christina Dodwell, fighting backwards down rapids

On the last rapids the expedition team struggle desperately to keep the boats from going under

The cutting went on for about fifteen minutes. My arm was bleeding profusely and I didn't watch the cuts because I didn't want to faint, but afterwards when they washed it I saw that it was a diamond-shaped mark with decorative fletchings. When it had been anointed with oil and ochre the men took me back into the *haus tamboran* for a small ceremony that gave me the highest honours they could bestow. It was similar to the British custom of giving the freedom of a city to someone; the villagers told me that through my initiation I had become an honorary member of the Sepik region, that in my future visits every door would be open to me and I would be free to enter the deeper mysteries of Sepik life.

On returning to the *Kaseli* I thought about the village *singsing* as I watched the christening of some new national converts, who were being baptised by immersion in the Sepik. When I asked the pastor about the meaning of baptism he said that Christians may not take part in any kind of traditional ritual or celebration, nor believe in the power of spirits or the *haus tamboran*, because such things are devil-worship.

Overzealous missions can cause irreparable damage; in some areas the missionaries have said that the old ways are evil, that wood-carvings are false idols, that dancing is not compatible with God, and they have been responsible for the burning down of many *haus tamborans*. But there is a positive side to the 'progress' brought by the missions; they are responsible for introducing health care, an awareness of the importance of nutrition, education and western ideas like motor-canoes; the pre-European environment was limited to the distance a man could paddle a canoe, and nowadays the outboard motor has opened up a new world. Similarly, transistor radios brought the villagers into contact with an even wider world and made people aware of their country.

The *Kaseli* had now completed its Sepik journey and its crew were ready to return to the coast. In total we had come about 250 miles up the Sepik; I was sad to say goodbye. But it was time for me to move on to the second stage of my journey: linking up with the Waghi River expedition to attempt a river yet more remote than this one. The expedition's starting-point was in the highlands so I made my way there by small plane.

From the air I could appreciate how the country's mountainous backbone was formed. When, millions of years ago, the mainland of palaeo-New Guinea drifted northwards and collided with an island arc, great chunks of the earth's crust, including the sea-floor, were thrust up vertically several miles. The tangle of steep, knife-edged ridges and deep, winding valleys are a sure sign of geological youthfulness. Originally the Waghi River flowed into the Sepik – until two million years ago when the volcano of Mount Hagen pushed its way up and changed the course of the Waghi, forcing it to run into the Tua River.

The first colonists thought that the highlands were unpopulated, until the 1930s and 1950s, when explorers found teeming populations of Stone-Age people. Even recently there have been discoveries of 'hidden valleys' whose tribes have not seen Europeans. These highlanders are not like the lowlanders with whom I was familiar; they are warrior-farmers and have little artistic culture or artefacts because they are too busy fighting for survival. Their only art is the painting and decoration of their bodies and faces in brightly coloured patterns to show their mood of well-being or aggression, displayed in *singsings* and in tribal warfare.

As planned, on 15 August I met the river-exploration team, which consisted of eight young Americans from Sobek, the foremost international company of white-water professionals. Adventure-seekers, they usually provide tourist trips but this time they were going to attempt the first descent of the Waghi River, to find out whether it was feasible and how far the river could be navigated.

'Sobek boatmen have rafted many of the world's wildest rivers, and already have several first descents to their credit,' said one of their most experienced boatmen, Mike Boyle, who was a tall, blond man with a drooping walrus moustache.

Their team was led by Skip Horner, along with Sobek's boss, Richard Bangs, and the boatmen were John Kramer, John Mason, Mike Boyle, Tim Whitney, Renée Goddard (the only woman other than myself), and the expedition's doctor, George Fuller. The doctor was a short, red-haired and gnomelike man; he replied to my enquiry about having brought pain-killers for emergencies by saying, 'I don't believe in using such things. After all, it's only pain, and you can't die from it.' I asked John Mason why he was doing the trip and he said, 'Because I love it. You haven't felt the exhilaration of whitewater, but you'll find out, I promise you.'

On 17 August we all assembled for the *singsing* and official send-off for our river expedition. The *singsing* opened with a dramatic entrance by warriors wearing head-dresses of tall, black feathers, and face-paints of white, red and yellow in startling patterns. The warriors marched in a column formation, stopping frequently to beat their drums and send out a vocal chant of oh-oh-oh drawn out in waves of rising excitement. The purpose of this display is to show off the men's strength, health and vigour. Their chests gleamed with pig-grease, some were blackened with charcoal all over their torsos, and for clothes they wore the leafy loin-cover known in Pidgin as *arse-grass*.

I sat on a raised bamboo platform beside Simon Koiam, the regional Premier, who was smartly dressed in a suit and tie; he spoke good English and while watching the warriors we talked about tribal warfare in his province. Battles occur because of land disputes or the stealing of pigs; warriors fight with bows and arrows and, although deaths are not common, the ancestor spirits require a pay-back killing of an enemy clansman. Last month two men were killed in fighting near Kundiawa, and Simon told me that the Government is trying to crack down on clan-fighting since it is illegal. He went on to say that actually he was only the Acting Premier, since the real Premier was away hiding from a pay-back death threat to his clan: a life for a life.

The *singsing* gathered momentum as the men made a charge across the cleared area brandishing spears, which they stopped just short of thrusting into Sobek's inflatable boats.

The following day I had my first experience of whitewater boating. Although 'whitewater' is the term used for long stretches of rapids, I wasn't worried, because the team's organiser assured me that this first day's trip would be an easy jaunt of 15 miles, simply to introduce me to some whitewater. Only two boats would be used instead of the usual three, and without the full crew of boatmen. As a boatman, my job was to help the boat to ride waves by pushing its nose down over the crests, and by paddling, bailing out water or 'hi-siding', which meant flinging myself onto the highest side of the boat if it was in danger of tipping upside-down. The oarsman was responsible for the speed and direction of the boat. Early in the morning we assembled on the Waghi river-bank near Moroma bridge. The task of inflating the boats with manual and foot pumps, attaching the metal frames, and arranging the luggage and supplies was a slow one; everything had to be tied on securely with special knots. Many willing hands helped move the inflatable boats down into the river, and when we set out the onlookers rushed onto the bridge to wave goodbye to us. I was sitting on the side-tube with a paddle in my hands while the oarsman sat in the centre of the boat. We floated gently along; water rippled under the soft rubber floor, and people chattered about river-currents and the small rapids ahead of us today.

The river valley was broad and fairly flat, open, grassy slopes, some cultivated patches of *kaukau* (sweet potato) and highland coffee grown by locals as a cash crop. There were small thatched huts on hilltops, fountains of bamboo, casuarina, mauve convolvulus entwining the tall reeds, and many butterflies. Approaching a gorge, the terrain became more mountainous and the river ran faster between banks of layered, volcanic rock. The first major rapids loomed close and we got ready to stop in an eddying pool by the shore so that the boatmen could scout the rapids for potential problems. But the river was too quick for us. Instead of catching the eddy, the boats were pulled into the rapids. The other boat surfed broadside over a swell and into the hollow trough or 'hole' where the violent, back-cycling action of waves began to swamp it. One oar was wrenched away and I glimpsed the strained, white faces of the crew, who were yelling with fear as our boat came over the swell and narrowly missed landing on top of them. The boats hit each other and ours went on out of control into the rapids. The other boat was still trapped by the back-cycling waves, and I saw people being swept out of the boat into the river.

The waves were 4 feet high, muddy brown splashed with foaming white, and their roar almost drowned out the shouts of alarm and panic, though I thought I heard someone yelling at me to hold on tightly. I redoubled my grip but I wasn't looking where we were going, my eyes were scanning the river behind us and for an agonising number of seconds nobody came up to the surface. It was terrifying to realise that they were in serious trouble. Then suddenly I saw a man in a red life-jacket being washed through the rapids behind us. As he came close to our boat I leaned out until he could grab my hands, and we pulled him into the boat. Looking up we saw two more struggling bodies being swept downstream, moving faster than our heavily-laden boat which bucked and ploughed its way on through the rapids. We bailed water out but more came in. I leaned out again to grab the arms of one of the swimmers and after he had been hauled into the boat we switched our attention to the other man, still in the river; he was panic-stricken and seemed to be injured. Despite his floundering efforts he was unable to reach our boat. Finally he was caught in an eddy and pushed to a rocky bank overhung with forest, where he staggered to the shore and collapsed. The current pulled our boat on through whitewater for another half-mile before we managed to catch an eddy and reach the shore. On board there was a frenzy of voices telling us what they had seen and what had happened, while others coughed up water and one gasped, 'I thought I was going to die. The force of water kept pushing me deeper, I couldn't breathe, I couldn't tell which way was upward, I thought the end had come.'

My heart was pounding with anxiety. The oarsman and the boat were still un-accounted for. The boat could still be trapped in the hole which someone explained was a keeper-hole; it could keep a boat or a human being underwater indefinitely. The idea was horrifying. I felt cold, wet and miserable.

After a long wait we sent out a search-party and waited for several hours before the boat arrived with its oarsman, and our search-party came back on foot along the river-bank with news that the injured man had been taken by local men to a jeep-track some miles away. We decided to continue onward in the boats to the road-bridge near Kundiawa, about 8 miles downriver.

The afternoon sky turned stormy as we paddled away and soon it was raining heavily. The gorge grew narrower and craggy cliffs rose vertically to both sides, towering above us, with tree-roots clinging tenuously for support to ledges of rock from which dripped formations of limestone stalactites. Mosses and ferns grew abun-dantly and there were caves and waterfalls. Soon our view was spoilt by another storm, thunder and lightning, and such torrential rain that we could only see a few feet ahead.

Sudden large waves indicated that we were in rapids again. I went cold with terror as we were pulled by the jostling current into waves 6 feet tall; we crested over a few and then I saw a hole much deeper than the one which had troubled us before. It was a 4-foot-deep oval trough just downsteam of a large rock, with brown waves fiercely back-cycling into its hollow. We slid past it, surfed the tail-waves and were clear of that section, bailing water frantically and facing more rapids just ahead. Rain was still lashing down, I was cold and depressed, and wondered about the wisdom of the whole journey. If this was my introduction to easy whitewater, I dreaded to think of the worse that was in store for us.

At Kundiawa we traced the injured man, who had reached a Catholic mission where he was treated for head injuries and shock by the local missionaries. 'Didn't you know,' they said, 'they call this river "The Eater of Men". They drag about one body a month out of the water near here.' The river is taking its revenge.

I carried a bucket down to the river for water. We were making our first campsite just 3 miles below the confluence of the Waghi and Asaro rivers, where the Waghi becomes known as the Tua. Our campsite was located on a boulder-strewn sandbank at a river-bend, backed by steep jungle. We had put our tents up at the far edge of the sandbank because, when it rains heavily in the river's headwaters, the river-level can rise dramatically fast and we didn't want our camp to be swept away.

The boatmen resecured the three boats in a small, rocky inlet, smooth, grey boats beside smooth, grey rocks. Having finished my chores, I sat on top of a tall rock and wrote my diary, and watched a flock of large, ungainly hornbilled cockamoors flying in to land on the branches of some trees. Unlike the Sepik's lowland trees, this was a cooler, mid-mountain forest with oaks and pines. Variety occurs because temperatures fall by about 3° for each 1000 feet of altitude; the apex of Papua New Guinea rises into misty cloud-forests and alpine moors. Here the forest was flourishing, tall, straight trees were draped with vines, looping lianas and creepers, while strangler vines had engulfed other tree-trunks in lethal, lacy patterns, and riverside trees were strung with aerial roots hanging down like tentacles toward the water.

At dusk we collected driftwood and built a fire to cook supper. I had expected to live off dried expedition supplies and was rather amazed to find that Sobek had brought an enormous amount of frozen meats including steaks, chops, chickens and oysters. Certainly this was no army expedition. We barbecued some T-bone steaks. Later, we sat around the fire and I listened while Skip, the team leader and oarsman for my boat, talked about his most difficult moments in the twelve years that he has been a boatman. All the Sobek people had good stories to tell, and as they talked I realised that since Sobek is a large organisation with many lists of boatmen, few of them had met each other or worked together before this trip. Sobek's boss, Richard Bangs, had hand-picked this group for our journey. Each was a distinct individual, with different strengths and qualities. They were warm, likeable people, and I felt hopeful they would soon be acting as a team, indeed they had been more careful since the shock of the accident. The future looked as if it would be enjoyable.

The next morning there were tedious and frustrating delays before we set out downriver, but my hot-and-bothered feeling was short-lived as within minutes we got soaked by waves spraying over the boat which was careering along in a foaming torrent. The first few miles seemed to be all rapids. My co-paddler, John Mason, was teaching me to throw my weight onto the prow as it crested on big waves, so that the boat didn't lose momentum or start sliding backwards. Oarsman Skip controlled our pace and direction, weaving a path through the rock-studded water. It wasn't alarming because, although we frequently got wet, the rapids were not large by international standards. John explained that there is an International Scale of Whitewater which measures the size of runnable rapids, numbering them from 1 to 5. One is easy and 5 almost too big to attempt; 6 to 10 are generally far too dangerous, but if easily laid out, a few can be runnable.

Hanging over the river we saw a vine bridge, about 30 yards long, suspended from platform gateways against the rugged cliffs. The bridge itself looked perilous, having gaps between the poles of the walkway, and its vine-rope sides were loosely knitted to form handrails. Further downriver we halted just before a big rapid while some boatmen went to scout a potential route through this 200-yard section. They came back and reported that it was class 5, just about runnable. With a river speed of 15 knots, the boats would need to go quickly to the other side, stay to the left, and then ride the tail-waves. We cast off from the shore but Skip's oar got jammed against something underwater. The oar bent alarmingly as the boat was dragged forward by the current; I was afraid of what could happen if the oar snapped, but suddenly it jerked free and we were away, rowing and paddling powerfully across the current to reach the river's left side. Our boat went well over the ledge, down the chute and into six big tail-waves; three of them were at least 10 feet high and came washing over the boat, whose front part filled up with water. One wave knocked me backwards but I grabbed the lifeline and held grimly onto my position. The sixth wave swung us

Even explorers with twentieth-century equipment are no match for the Waghi

around backwards but Skip didn't seem worried, and soon we reached a calm patch where we busily bailed water out of the boat. The next rapid caught us in a 'monster eddy' whose eye managed to suck down one side of the boat until water poured in, so we 'hi-sided' to balance the boat and it came free, which was a relief. Sudden dangers and shocks were making me realise how unpredictable a river can be, forcing me to give it respect.

At noon we parked under a tree with tentacle-like aerial roots; George the doctor dislocated his shoulder while swinging from one of them, and Renée fell backwards over an oar, but both accidents were easily remedied. Already on our journey we had met with our share of scratches and bruises. But so far I'd been lucky.

The afternoon brought much whitewater in a narrow, rocky gorge among mountains whose peaks were 1000 feet above us, rising up against a stormy, grey sky. At one bend in the valley the current surged strongly against a cliff-wall, and our boat was pulled straight towards it. 'Look out,' yelled John as we slammed nose first into the wall; the boat reared up, flipped over sideways, and fell upside-down. I fell with it; the river closed over my head as the current dragged me downwards and churned me around underwater like a rag doll. Fortunately I had taken a breath of air, so I shut my eyes and made myself relax. Within seconds I came up to the surface, floating buoyantly into more rapids. The upturned boat was just ahead of me, and I was able to catch up with it and cling onto the lifeline. Skip and John were also holding on for dear life, and I could see another boat heading to rescue us. In the meantime we managed to haul ourselves on top of our upturned boat as it sped through a canyon. Then I heard the roaring of more rapids ahead. Quickly I searched for handholds but the upturned boat offered none, so I stood up to get a better view of what we were in for and my heart plummeted. Rocks, back-cycling holes – I thought we were doomed.

Shouts echoed between the canyon's bare limestone walls as the second boat picked Tim out of the water and threw a rope towards our boat. The boats drew together, the whitewater was also approaching but the two boats were close enough for me to jump between them so long as I didn't misjudge the distance. As we entered the rapids I checked the gap and leapt toward the second boat, landing squarely on the front tube.

The boat was crowded now with six on board, a heavy load for Mike to row, but for the moment I felt safe. Mike was heading for a break in the gorge where we could catch an eddy, to eddy out. More shouts echoed between the cliffs as John was swept off the upturned boat, and again as Skip hauled him back onto it.

The rescue boatmen had got hold of the upturned boat's bowline, and suddenly it pulled tight across us. With cries of alarm, people scattered to avoid injury and I ducked to the floor. Mike strained at the oars in desperation, rowing the weight of the two boats, and as the eddy came near he stood and threw all his strength against the oars.

We caught the eddy and two men leapt for shore with the boats' bowlines; then they battled to pull the boats out of the current. Quickly securing the bowlines to rocks they set about righting the upturned boat, using a rock as a pivot. When it flipped back I noticed with surprise that nothing had fallen out, so securely had it all been tied in.

With dry land under my feet I felt safe again. Although I was shaken, this certainly had not been the most frightening experience of my life, but I counted myself lucky to have escaped so easily.

Rain began falling heavily, but it would soon clear. I walked up the bank and found a wide, raised expanse of sand protected from the river by huge boulders, and with a pond of clear water in the sand, an idyllic campsite. We had a good night's sleep, but our problems hadn't ended.

The next day we reached an impassable rapid. Skip and I walked along the rocky shore and he explained how he 'reads' a rapid: this one was class 7. It had about twelve major drops over a distance of half a mile, and although each individual drop was technically feasible, the combination of them was probably lethal. It was unrunnable.

Thus we were faced with a porterage that would be made extremely difficult by the valley's steep sides. Twentieth-century technology came to our rescue in the shape of a helicopter which carried our inflated boats away downriver one by one in make-shift slings. The helicopter hovered just above us while we attached the boats because there was no possible landing space on the rocks, and when my turn came to board the helicopter it hovered with one skid on a rock while I grabbed the other skid to help me climb up the rock and get into the passenger seat. The pilot was a Vietnamese war veteran, experienced in such exercises.

We flew over ten parts of the rapid and touched down just before the final stages of whitewater, which the Sobek crew wanted to attempt by boat. I looked at the rapids and the heaving, foaming chaos of 15-foot waves and 10-foot holes. I felt worried. There was no doubt that the river was getting stronger and dropping more steeply; the rapids were continually growing bigger, and the waves which had once seemed big at 6 feet were now paltry in comparison with what we were tackling.

The boats were ready to run and, as usual, our boat would lead the way. We took the left side, sliding between two rocks and into enormous, 12-foot waves which soaked us as they poured over the boat. I gripped the boat, determined not to be swept off it, only letting go to do some quick bailing of water. At the second major drop-down one of Skip's oar fixtures slipped. We struggled to remove the oar and replace the fixture with the spare one, while avoiding the river's obstacles, which we achieved without mishap.

Behind us, Richard Bangs' boat went nose first into a hole but surfed through it onto the recycling wave-crest, where the boat spun broadside and came close to sliding back into the hole. Richard rowed hard and the boat came bucking its way downriver. Mike, rowing the third boat, looked to be well in control.

On the following four days we ran a lot of whitewater and covered a fair number of miles, and in one day we achieved 50 miles. They were days of anxiety, fear, frustrating hassles and hardships, balanced by awe, joy, serenity and fun. On calmer stretches of river Skip gave me rowing lessons.

Frequently we passed waterfalls cascading down the river-banks, some of which had eroded their way backwards to form narrow canyons and circular pools whose white cliffs dripped luxuriant green mosses and ferns. By walking upstream we found other falls, breathtakingly beautiful with multilevel scalloped limestone bowls, overflowing in cascades to lower pools.

At various moments I had the startling realisation of being where no European had ever set foot. Certainly no European had descended the Tua River, although fifty years ago a pair of Australians, Leahy and Dwyer, on a gold-prospecting expedition, came south on foot beside a tributary of the Tua. They were attacked by Kukukuku (a notorious tribe of savage killers known for their cannibal habits) with stone war-clubs but they managed to follow the river to the coast. Other prospectors, such as Naylor and Clarius, were killed by them. It seems that they killed for the easy meat, unlike head-hunters who have more spiritual reasons, such as to celebrate the baptism of a young child. Other highland clans practised cannibalism to gain the strength of the slain, and the Fores did it out of love, believing that unless this ritual was followed the spirit would not get free from the body, and it would be condemned to eternal limbo. Unfortunately for the Fores, the decomposing flesh was often contaminated by *Kuru* (Laughing Death), a fatal disease carried only by humans. The continued occurrence of *Kuru* shows that the old ways are still in existence.

We came to some rock headlands where the river narrowed to 50 feet with swirling back-currents. It was hard paddling through the gateway, but beyond it we entered a calm gorge of sculpted limestone, with long fingers of rock jutting out of the water.

The raft is swept perilously near the rocky banks of the river

'Where did that come from?' yelled John as we rocked in a sudden turbulence of underwater currents which boiled up to the surface and made raised domes of water; but they were no great threat to us. Later, I felt some trepidation when we got caught in fast shallows and our boat went out of control and was scraped over sharp rocks sideways. We were swept over a 3-foot ledge, landed amongst rough waves and made haste to the centre channel where more enormous waves rolled us along. My nervousness turned to a glorious excitement. The jungle rang with bird screeches and cicadas, the waves roared, and sometimes people yelped with alarm or joy.

One day I made a side-trip to a collection of huts called Kokea and during my visit the headman, Giami, took me to see the bodies of his ancestors. It was a place that I had heard about during my travels in the highlands in 1980, but although I had been given directions how to reach it then this was the first chance I'd had to visit it. It had been described as a sacred place of ancestors with a line of smoke-preserved corpses or mummies sitting beside a cliff.

The walk to the cliff rose steeply uphill and I gasped for breath, but Giami trod effortlessly and told me, '*Mi sori, wokabaut bilong yumi stap longwei liklik.*' (Sorry, our walk is a little further.)

We rounded a rocky outcrop and suddenly I was on a crumbly ledge below an overhanging cliff. Just in front of me was a line of about ten smoked corpses, sitting with their knees drawn up to their chests, held above ground by a row of open baskets propped up on poles. Giami said that most of the bodies had been here for

Christina Dodwell with a corpse at Kokea. To preserve the bodies of their great warriors the villagers smoked the corpses over wood-fires and later put them up in the mountains

centuries, although some were more recent and he pointed to one shrunken body which he said was brought here fourteen years ago. Its dry, red-ochred skin was shrivelled, and looked like parchment; its skull was propped up by an arrow and its empty eye-sockets stared out at the world.

According to Giami, the man had been a *bigman* called Moaymungo, and after his death his family had smoke-cured his corpse for several months in a smoke-house, like a ham, before carrying it up to its place here. People believe that the ancestor-spirits watch over their descendants and protect them. The idea of burying the dead in the ground has now been introduced by the Government, and the smoking of corpses is illegal.

It was a spooky place, but somehow the bodies were not a gruesome or macabre sight. The tranquillity here was almost tangible. As I stood and rested among the mummies, I gave thanks for life and travel, feeling privileged to be there, at peace with the world and with the daily unfolding of my journey.

For most of our nights beside the Tua we camped on raised sandy beaches, beautiful campsites, but on two nights the water-level rose until the camp had to be moved. The second time, I woke up as water lapped into my tent. There were yells of agitation from outside and I hurriedly joined the throng of sleepy people moving their tents and bedding to higher ground.

The following morning we packed up camp and loaded the boats in record time.

74

We had become a well-co-ordinated team, and despite our tiredness and ailments everyone was in good humour. Most of the team had foot-rot, infected insect bites, stomach problems, fevers, and gashes and bruises from falling on slippery rocks. A feeling of nervousness stayed with me all that morning as we led the way downriver, negotiating the current and swinging between craggy limestone banks, the water boiling up and sucking downward in eddies. We paused to scout a big rapid. 'Holy Moses!' exclaimed several of the men when they saw the size of the whitewater. Its first steep drop had twin cascading waterfalls parted by a giant tongue of water falling into a turmoil of back-cycling waves. Almost immediately, the river turned sharply left and went into a similar but bigger drop-down with many massive tail-waves. Its force was frightening.

I asked Richard how this rapid measured against other big ones and he said that frankly it was off the scale of runnable rapids. In steepness and power it was far larger than a class 10 rapid, yet in formation it wasn't technically complex. John Kramer added that it's rare to find a rapid with such drop and volume that is in any way runnable. This one was technically runnable.

The news sent a shiver down my spine. None of the team had ever tackled anything this size. Everyone was given the choice of attempting to run the rapid or walking along the rocks and meeting the boats again after the rapid. Some of the team preferred to walk. They thought that if a boat was going to be eaten by the river, it was likely to happen here. I fully realised that we would be lucky to come out in one piece, but there was no question in my mind: if my boat crew were willing to tackle it, I was game to try.

The anxiety was fearful; we were first to go, and Skip rowed us out into the raging current, pulling hard to angle the boat toward the left-hand chute. Then he stopped rowing and his face showed a calm readiness; no point in rowing now, we were in perfect alignment. The current took us down the tongue and into the throat where V-waves converged; suddenly waves were breaking 20 feet above us, crashing over and into us until the boat seemed to be underwater. 'Inflatable boats can't sink,' I kept telling myself, and it was true because the boat's rim bobbed up a fraction and we began to move again, while we bailed like crazy as our boat rode the series of massive waves.

From the crest of a wave I saw Mike Boyle's boat heading for the left side of the tongue but he cut it too fine and they plummeted backward over the waterfall, straight into the vortex of the hole. Mike was catapulted out of his boat into the back-cycling hole. He came to the surface but was pulled underwater again. Their boat was still intact; George the doctor lunged toward the oars but at that instant the boat flipped upside-down. I lost sight of everything as we were pulled into the second half of the rapid, which was bigger and much wilder that the first. Over the tongue, into a side vortex, a whirling mass of water and 25-foot waves; several times I thought our boat was going to flip upside-down; we alternately hi-sided or threw our weight on the nose, and got through; but it was an awesome experience.

Below the rapids we caught an eddy and stopped by some rocks. Boat 3 managed to rescue Mike, but George and Renée swam the second half of the rapid. Renée successfully climbed onto the upturned boat, and when it collided with a rock not far from the shore, she jumped onto it. George drifted to shore in an eddy, looking none the worse for his swim, but Renée looked badly shaken.

We stayed to collect them while boat 3 went in pursuit of the upturned boat 2. If they didn't catch up with it before the next big rapid, the boat would probably be lost. John Kramer, in boat 3, rowed like a man possessed. Skip's boat followed some way behind, going more slowly through the canyon whose limestone cliffs rose sheer above us for hundreds of feet. At water-level there were caves and overhangs of fossilised sea-bed rocks. The lower end of this gorge is called Hathor Gorge, named after the mythical cow-headed goddess Hathor whose beauty was reputed to cause death.

The canyon widened slightly at a bend, and beside its sandy beach we saw the two boats. We made camp and relived the day's dramas, and I realised how much I'd grown to like these people. Mike talked about his fall and getting swirled underwater so violently that he thought he would drown. Renée had been trapped under the upturned boat, unable to find air, but she had fought her panic and groped her way out, determined not to drown.

After breakfast the next morning we began to scout the next rapid ahead of us. It came as a shock to discover that it was totally unrunnable; its formation would demand impossible manoeuvres and if a boat capsized there were many instant death-traps for swimmers. The sheer cliffs made it impossible to make a porterage around the rapid, and even if we had bypassed that one, there were yet bigger rapids stretching for many miles down the gorge.

The power of this river was far greater than even the experts had expected. It is not navigable. By pushing ourselves and the boats to the limits we had, in two arduous weeks, come such a long way. We were now within 20 miles of where the Tua becomes the Purari. I had loved the river and its whitewater, and it was almost unbearable to think that the expedition was over. Things seemed to be happening too fast, I wasn't yet ready for the end. But a day later we began the laborious business of getting airlifted out.

As I flew by helicopter away from the river I was consoled by the thought that this had been only my first taste of whitewater, and it had certainly unfolded new horizons for me. In my journey I had managed to see places that no one else has reached, and to visit remote villages where little has changed since history began – spirit houses, skin-cutting, crocodile hunting, smoked corpses and initiation rites. Our expedition had not opened the river to the twentieth century, but perhaps that was the best outcome. I was reminded of the words of an earlier traveller, written only thirty years ago. 'This is a last brave land. As lush with challenge as with wild, green growth, it throws a gauntlet in our civilised faces – a whole uncivilisation of untamed terrain and untamed people.'

THE MEKONG

William Shawcross

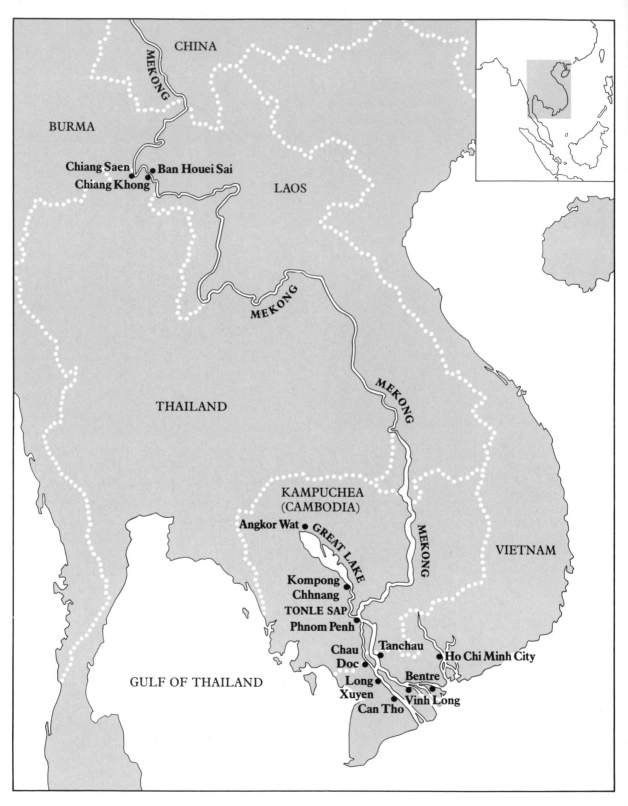

CHINA

BURMA

MEKONG

Chiang Saen
Chiang Khong
Ban Houei Sai

LAOS

MEKONG

THAILAND

MEKONG

KAMPUCHEA
(CAMBODIA)

Angkor Wat
GREAT LAKE

MEKONG

VIETNAM

Kompong
Chhnang

TONLE SAP

Phnom Penh

Chau
Doc
Tanchau

Ho Chi Minh City

Long
Xuyen
Can Tho

Bentre

Vinh Long

GULF OF THAILAND

My first day on the river, rather to my surprise, I was taken to see the sea. It was the idea of Comrade Long, the Representative for Cultural Affairs on the Administrative Committee of the Province of Bentre. This is one of the southern provinces of Vietnam, through which the Mekong rushes in thousands of streams and rivers finally to end its long journey from Tibet by debouching, in nine large floods known as the Dragon's Mouths, into the South China Sea.

Comrade Long and his superiors thought that before I went upstream I should see some 'seashore activities'; I have always loved the sea and did not demur. Through no fault of theirs we were late in setting off. By the time we arrived at a village near one of the Dragon's Mouths, it was nearly dusk and the sky was grey with rain. Boats were steaming back home with the day's shrimp catch, and men were carrying baskets of fish and shrimps ashore. Outside the bamboo huts and in the little market-place women were sorting the catch; babies were being swung high in hammocks to make them sleep. Despite the hour, Comrade Long – no sailor – strode off to find the head of the village committee to arrange a boat to take me towards the ocean. I wandered around on my own.

It was a pretty place on a tributary, still well inside the river's mouth – the sort of village from which, I imagined, later at night boats, heavily laden not with shrimps but with people, had for years been slipping quietly away into the dark sea, bound for Thailand, Malaysia or Hong Kong. Since 1978 about half of Vietnam's entire fishing fleet has sailed away. So have about half a million people. We finally set off on an old wooden fishing-boat, unpainted for years, with a graceful line and a high deck-house. It might have carried 300 refugees; now there were fewer than a dozen of us on board, on an excursion and not a flight. It was an uncomfortable feeling.

A fishing-boat at the mouth of the Mekong Delta

After we had been sailing for about half an hour towards the sea, I suddenly heard shots from the bank. They were not being fired directly at us, but they were fired on account of us nonetheless. Warning shots across the bow, so to speak. At once the captain put the helm hard over and we steamed fast towards the shore where a police post was situated. On a falling tide, we ran on to the mud about 200 yards from the beach. Policemen came and told us we were under arrest – the first British boat people, I suppose. It was midnight before the unfortunate Comrade Long was able to clear up the problem and have us released.

I had first visited Vietnam in 1970. There were still hundreds of thousands of US troops there, but their numbers were gradually being reduced by President Nixon as the war effort was 'Vietnamised' – an ugly phrase which reflected L.B.J.'s slogan, 'Asian Boys to fight Asian Wars'. I had found both Vietnam and Cambodia, which had just begun its headlong fall into its own unique form of hell on earth, intensely moving, and from 1970 onwards I had tried to return as often as possible. That, however, was not very often and, unlike wiser, more adventurous or braver people, I had never lived in either place. I wish I had. After the Communist victories in 1975 I had not been able to obtain visas to enter either country until 1980.

When in October 1983 I stepped once more off the weekly Air France flight to the town which is now called Ho Chi Minh City but still feels much like Saigon, I would tell a lie if I did not say that I was thrilled to bits. I had come to make a BBC film on the Mekong and I was met by not one but four officials of Hanoi Television; they seemed delightful. At the edge of the airport, in the days of President Thieu, there had been a concrete slab which read: 'The noble sacrifice of allied soldiers will never be forgotten.' The slab was still there, but the promise had been painted out. My guides took me to the hotel, suggested I have lunch upstairs and arranged to meet me later. Instead I went out into the streets.

The town was much quieter than during the war; no armoured cars, no jeeps, fewer motor vehicles of all kinds, many more bicycles, and scores of bicycle rickshaws or 'cyclos'. There were children selling cigarettes and peanuts. On the pavements, as before, squatted women wearing the traditional Vietnamese conical straw hats and selling snacks. Everyone smiled at me; I had forgotten how much people do smile in Vietnam. In the middle of the street were booths where, in the last days of the war, Vietnamese had frantically made photocopies of their papers in the hope of persuading the Americans to take them out. Now some of the booths were empty, while others sold baskets and lacquerware.

I had not gone far when, to my surprise, I heard a cry: 'William! William!' It was the young driver of a bicycle rickshaw whom I had met on my last trip in 1981. He was still wearing the shirt I had given him then. I was delighted to see him, and we cycled off to lunch in a Vietnamese café some blocks away, where we ate a delicious meal of fish soup, prawns and chicken – it would have cost about three months' wages at the official, and largely disregarded, rate of exchange between dollars and Vietnamese dong, but at the unofficial rate it was a great deal less. As we finished, a crowd of children and an old man clustered around the table, begging to be allowed to take away the remains in bowls which they carried.

Back at the hotel the guides from Hanoi TV invited me to the upstairs restaurant and we talked about the journey. One of them, named Mr Hong, was a producer and he described himself as 'No. 1 fixer'. A very cheerful man, filled with energy, he was always darting around, filled with new ideas. His principal colleague, who would be with us all the way, was a woman called Tuc. She was both beautiful and graceful. Her hair was cut short and she wore simple slacks and a shirt. Her smile suggested both kindness and wit, and she had infinite patience. Among the various other officials was a man who was also with us throughout our journey, but gave us no help at all. His purpose seemed to be to take notes on Tuc and what she did for us. Another, who did not travel with us, told me that after my last trip some people in Vietnam had criticised my articles. This time I must remember that they would be held responsible for what I wrote and for the film. I noticed that at the next table sat a man with his back to the guides. Occasionally he would lean back in his chair and say something to them.

The plans seemed fine. We would travel by car from Ho Chi Minh City to Bentre and then, so far as possible, up or along the river to the Cambodian border. Mr Hong would fly to Phnom Penh, the capital of Cambodia (or Kampuchea, as it is now known), to arrange our journey there. Since the Cambodian authorities were installed and maintained in power by Vietnamese divisions, I thought there would be few problems.

'But what about Laos?' I asked. After the Delta and Cambodia, the river winds up through Laos, Thailand, Laos and Thailand again, before skirting Burma and disappearing into China and home to Tibet. Back in 1981 or certainly 1982, the Lao Embassy in London had at once given me a visa. But, in an apparent display of independence from their Vietnamese overlords, the Laos had withdrawn this as soon as the Vietnamese adopted the project.

'Don't worry,' I was told. 'Everything will be fixed for Laos. We are having discussions with their embassy in Hanoi.'

'Fine,' I said.

That evening I set off again into the streets. I was rather mournfully searching for a girl whom I had met in 1981. She was determined to take a boat and get away, she had said; her father had been imprisoned without trial in a re-education camp since 1975. She could not stand it here and had already tried twice to become a boat person, but each time she had been arrested and held by the Vietnamese police until she bought her release. We had sat in a café which, in the American days, had been a bar, while the hi-fi played a song by Boney M:

> I see a boat on the river,
> It's sailing away,
> Down to the ocean,
> Where to, I can't say.

I had tried to persuade her that the dangers of the ocean, especially of Thai pirates who freely rob and rape the people on Vietnamese refugee boats, were so great that she should not take the risk; she had said I was wrong, that anything was better than living under the Communists. She had promised to write if and when she arrived; in thirty months I had had no letter. Nor could I find her that first evening back in Ho Chi Minh City.

I went to the Seamen's Club, simply walking past the sentries at the dock gates and along the side of the wharf past the towering bulwarks of Polish, Cuban and Romanian ships. The club, for foreign sailors only, is built like a Japanese garden on the side of the dock. Little bridges lead over empty concrete streams. The garden contains some cages in which a couple of tacky monkeys and a moth-eaten bear swing and prowl. They are not the only wildlife. As I sat at a table in the garden I watched, without concentrating, a large rat run along a low wall towards me. It was only when it actually jumped on to my trousers that I awoke to its reality, and leapt to my feet. At that moment I was glad of the plague jab which had ruined a weekend for me.

A band was playing western rock music, loudly and badly. There were girls for the sailors to dance with, but they looked more painted and more miserable than I recalled. Sharp at 10 p.m. they were loaded into a ramshackle bus and driven out of the port – not like in the days of the puppet regime.

The sailors in the club that night were mostly Polish and mostly sloshed – on Vietnamese vodka and Bulgarian Blanc de Blancs. The Poles did not speak much English but they were very friendly and they made it clear that they were very keen on Lech Walesa and his Nobel Peace Prize. They invited me back on board, but I foresaw more vodka, more Blanc de Blancs, more incomprehensible camaraderie; so I declined, and returned to the hotel.

The Majestic is a lovely old building by the river with a number of vast and glittering suites redolent of the old colonial days. Even the lifts at the Majestic have charm: they have doors which you can open when the car itself is several floors below. Late at night after too many Vietnamese 'La Rue' beers – '*La bière La Rue/La bière qui tue*' goes the doggerel – this can prove hazardous. The latest victim was said to be an East German engineer.

The food in the Majestic is not good, but that is unimportant because the restaurant is situated on the top floor. I could sit at my table and watch as, beyond the port, the great ships wound their way on the invisible river through the paddy-fields. They looked like cardboard cut-outs in a children's game.

In the street outside the hotel were clusters of pathetic half-caste kids, the offspring of American fathers and Vietnamese mothers. 'Children of the dust', as they are sometimes called, they have been discriminated against by the regime and forgotten by the Americans. Now they court the sympathy of foreigners. Bill, about sixteen and with sandy hair, came up to me first. Pressing a tiny packet of peanuts into my hand he said, 'I Bill, my father American, my mother Vietnamese.'

'Do you like living in Vietnam?' I asked him.

'No, this winter I go America to my father,' he replied.

'Where in America?' I asked.

'United States,' he said.

He pointed out his mother, selling cigarettes by the road. She was now fat, shapeless and middle-aged, and it was hard to think of her as a svelte bar girl attending to the needs of GIs. Our cameraman, Alan Stevens, was very kind to Bill and later, back in England, he received a letter from him saying, 'You are my father now.'

As I was about to leave the hotel to start my journey, I met a Dutch film crew in the foyer. They were fussing and filming around a shy, diminutive teenage girl called Kim Phuoc. Poor Kim Phuoc! I will explain.

One morning back in 1972 I had hired one of the large taxis that plied from the Continental Hotel to take reporters on day-trips to the war. For weeks we had been going up Route 13 where the North Vietnamese had laid siege to the town of An Loc and the fighting had been particularly bloody. That day I thought I would have a rest from the endless fire-fights and go instead up Route 1 to Tay Ninh, where the Cao Dai monks practised their religion in a curious temple which included monuments to Sun Yat Sen, Victor Hugo and Winston Churchill.

It was like any other day's drive through the war. Once we were free of the confused bustle and noise of Saigon, the road ran through little villages where stalls were piled high with fruit. Water-buffalo grazed in the fields while helicopter gunships prowled the sky above, and American and South Vietnamese strike helicopters dived at targets beyond the tree-line. The car stopped unexpectedly among others outside the little village of Trang Bang. We did not know why. A few hundred yards ahead, a plume of smoke was rising listlessly from around the spire of a church.

Then we saw an old woman stumbling down the road with a child in her arms. The child seemed lifeless. Its skin was peeling from its body in thick layers, like paper. I learned that several journalists, including one from the BBC, had been pouring water over another child who was shivering with terror. It was Kim Phuoc.

We learned that a South Vietnamese war-plane had accidentally dropped napalm on the pagoda at Trang Bang; these children were among those seared in its flames and had run screaming out of the village. It was a horrible incident, but not particularly unusual. What made it exceptional was that, as the children ran down the road, they had been photographed by a Vietnamese photographer, Nick Ut. Millions of appalling pictures were taken in Vietnam, but for some reason this one of a little naked girl, screaming as she ran, captured attention and concern throughout the western world. With such publicity, Kim Phuoc was guaranteed the best medical attention available in South Vietnam and, although she was very badly scarred, she survived.

Now, in 1983, the Communist authorities had suddenly produced Kim Phuoc, partly to offset claims that the little girl had become a boat person and was now living in California. Instead of being allowed to live in decent obscurity she was again becoming a celebrity, compelled to rehearse her memories ceaselessly and to display her gnarled back for western photographers and cameramen. The Dutch producer, who was behaving towards her like a charming uncle, showed me big blown-up photographs of her in hospital in 1972 and recovering afterwards. She was being fondled by a German photographer with long hair and a long moustache. I was moved to meet her, but I found something bizarre in the way in which western journalists, both at the time and now, wanted to be near her, to touch her, to claim a part of her, to be photographed with her, to seize a particle of her life to enliven their own personal biographies.

I said goodbye and we set off for the river, careering along in a minibus into the gorgeous green which is so much a part of my memories of Vietnam, a green so much more striking and startling than that of England, and especially lush now because the year's main rice crop was growing tall in the paddies, ripe for harvest.

The actual river journey began later that day in the Dragon's Mouths with our inauspicious arrest as boat people. The next morning, after our eventual release, Comrade Long took me to the Bentre port to board a large boat belonging to the Committee. The dockside was crowded with boats – long wooden passenger-boats taking people up or downriver, and small sampans (which are like large canoes) on which peasants had brought their vegetables, ducks and pigs to sell in the busy, noisy, colourful market. But the boat on which I was to spend the day had none of the vitality of the others: it was a large official launch. I was to visit a sugar-refinery, the home of a heroine of the revolution and 'victims of defoliation'. These were all scenes which Comrade Long and the Committee thought were appropriate parts of my journey. They were not so keen on my meeting ordinary people whom they had not preselected.

During the war US planes had dropped hundreds of thousands of tons of chemicals on the forests of Vietnam in order to destroy the Communists' ground cover. One of the most destructive substances was called Agent Orange; it contained dioxin. Many Vietnamese doctors and officials are convinced – as are many American veterans – that Agent Orange is having long-term effects on the people who were exposed to it. In the United States veterans have pursued successful lawsuits against the companies which produced the chemical. In Vietnam it is being blamed for deformities in children. Undoubtedly it was an atrocious weapon.

Our boat, which carried a rather large number of young men in clean white shirts – which I had by now recognised as the badge of the plain-clothes policeman – eventually nosed its way into the river-bank, at a place where the palm-trees gave way to a small clinic which served villages in the forest back from the bank. Here Comrade Long had gathered people who were supposed to be victims of chemical warfare. I am sure that many had genuinely suffered from the horror. They were mostly elderly and told stories of being sprayed by the noxious fluids and of the awful effects this had upon their lives and their health. There was also a man carrying his young son, who had a deformed ankle. The father's story was that in 1969 the young girl who was to be his wife had been in an area which was sprayed. They had since had three children: two of them were fine but this child, the middle one, had been born with the deformity, in 1977.

The link between the defoliation and the child's deformity seemed to me to be tenuous in this case. Such deformities can be seen all over Asia and Africa and usually have more to do with vitamin deficiency than with poison. Nonetheless, after discussing it, we decided to film the poor child. He began to scream, begging his father to take him home, pointing to the way they had come, hours ago, to wait for us. It was deeply upsetting. He had been brought here to satisfy the Party's propaganda requirements, but also to satisfy the requirements of western film-making. His father said we were the seventh foreign film crew to whom the boy had been displayed. I should have refused to film him at all, and then perhaps Comrade Long would have decided his presence was not necessary the next time. As it was, by agreeing to treat him as a 'victim of defoliation', I contributed to making him a freak

A rice farmer and his child in the Mekong Delta

as well as a cripple. Afterwards I sat on the boat cursing myself and the policemen and officials who surrounded us – but especially myself.

Hundreds of people take the river to Bentre every day. Some of the passenger-boats make journeys of a whole day's stretch. I wanted to take one of the bigger boats upstream to Vinh Long, the capital of the neighbouring province, but we would then come into contact with ordinary travellers and this was not a prospect that Comrade Long and his companions viewed with much pleasure. They wanted to choose the people to whom I talked and suggested that I travel in secure isolation on board an empty boat which the Committee would provide. Fortunately, our patient guide Tuc understood what I wanted. For hour after hour she explained and negotiated with Comrade Long *et al* and eventually, thanks to her alone, I found myself walking through the market full of pigs, rice, chickens and vegetables – the produce of the verdant Delta – and about to start along the river road to China.

The boat, long and of unpainted wood, was almost all cabin; there was a small deck up front and a poop with a charcoal fire for the crew's lunch and a lavatory for anyone small enough to squeeze into it and squat above a hole in the floor. Above the clattering engine was a box which served as a large bunk where, it seemed, one lucky member of the crew and his girlfriend were enjoying each other most of the day.

The boat, which carried both passengers and freight, belonged to a middle-aged Sino-Vietnamese woman. She had quite a number of her family aboard and gave sharp orders to the crew. Many of the passengers were peasants travelling only a few miles home upstream, having sold their produce in town. On the flat roof were half a dozen goats which a young man was taking for sale up the river; he would get a better price for them there, he said. Sitting on the roof near him were two pretty young women who laughed uproariously for a time – until two of my officious young police escorts, whom I disliked, snarled something at them. After that, whenever the police were around they put on serious faces and would not look at me. But when the police went below they began to smile again and even to make crude gestures of contempt after them.

I struck up conversation with one boy who spoke good French and some English. He came from Kontum, a lovely town in the highlands, a place of tigers, orchids and cool breezes. His parents were still there, he said, though retired now. (Often 'retirement' is a euphemism for the fact that work is denied because of connections with the puppet regime.) In due course the boy went off about his business. Next time I tried to talk to him he shook his head, motioning towards the policeman behind me. He then went below deck. The policeman followed and spoke to him very sharply. The boy cowered and retired to the stern where he remained for the rest of the day.

Left: the boat William Shawcross took from Bentre to Vinh Long. Above: William Shawcross and passengers on the boat to Vinh Long

All the way along the river we stopped to pick up or drop off passengers or goats – sometimes at villages, and sometimes at clearings in the forest on the bank. As the afternoon came down a monsoon storm engulfed the boat. Wooden shutters were fixed into all the open holes which constituted windows, and the cabin became almost dark; the engine noise increased to a roar, and the rain slashed in through the gaps. The only window left open was that through which the helmsman, perched on his rickety chair, tried to peer. He was soaked within a few minutes, even though they put a half-pane of broken yellow glass in the window and gave him a plastic mac to wear. Everyone came inside except for the goatherd on the roof. Bizarrely but kindly, he stood there trying in vain to give his goats some shelter from the storm under a sheet of plastic. Eventually this was too much and he brought his goats down below; they came tumbling down the stairs, shit a lot and munched at the stalks of a bunch of coconuts on the floor.

Perhaps because of the dark, the girls from the poop had cheered up immensely. One was flirting with great gusto with Alan, our cameraman; both of them exchanged addresses with me. One of them stuffed my card into her bra, sticking her tongue out at the back of a policeman as she did so and then bursting into laughter which was echoed by two of the youngest boat boys, bubbles of laughter both of them. The elder of the two was soaked through by the storm and shivering. He gestured at my shirt; later, on the roof, making sure that no policemen were watching me, I gave him a T-shirt from my bag. He seized it and scampered off down the deck to hide it before a policeman saw him.

The helmsman at the wheel during the storm

By the time the storm abated evening was coming down; the sun broke briefly through the clouds and then disappeared behind the palms. In the distance we could now see the lights of Vinh Long across a broad stretch of water. The boat was brought alongside the wharf near the market. It had been a wonderful day, and with regret I said goodbye to the crew, who were to sleep aboard and who would return next day to Bentre. Then I walked across to the very modern and luxurious Tourist Hotel, which had apparently just opened for business.

After supper I took a long cyclo ride along the quiet lanes beside a tributary of the Mekong. As I sat in comfort, being pedalled furiously by a silent driver, we passed only a few people walking home in the dark. I found a little café in an ordinary house, with a number of young men sitting at the tables. No one seemed surprised to see me. I had a beer. The owner said quietly he was sorry not to welcome me better: '... *le gouvernement socialiste, m'sieur.*' My cyclo driver was gone now, so I walked back into town; there I found a little street full of stalls, each of which was a café and each of which was lit by a flickering paraffin lamp. I had a soda and it was delightful: I felt a sense of tranquillity that is impossible to find when surrounded by police. I thought that southern Vietnam now seemed a totally different country from that of ten years ago. The surface brashness and vulgarity had all but disappeared, the veneer of commerce had gone. I thought that perhaps one might say that Vietnam had sunk back into the obscurity and calm from which it should never have emerged. But then I thought again that would not be true. There is the continued Vietnamese occupation of Cambodia for one thing, and the fact that so many hundreds of thousands of people have chosen to flee their country belies any idea of calm. Furthermore, I thought, how far was I any more able now to know what was really going on, what people were really thinking, where their actual loyalties were, than any wretched US army officer or civilian adviser?

The next morning I went by car to Can Tho, the capital city of the Delta, and once one of the biggest US bases in the area. To reach it we had to cross another branch of the Mekong on a rusty old car ferry packed with ancient buses and trucks, vendors of pineapples and cigarettes, farmers carrying upside-down ducks and hens, laughing schoolchildren, a few army officers, and a helmsman who spun the great wheel very expertly with his big toe.

In Can Tho I went to a charming little café – part in a garden, part in the colonnade of a house – where students and young workers come in the evenings, sit on low stools, drink sweet black coffee, very cheap, and listen to music, both western and Vietnamese. Later in the day I came back, but now it was packed with those young men in clean white shirts. Two of them tried to stop me talking to someone they had not selected, and I regret to say I lost my temper, complaining that I had come to Vietnam to talk to ordinary people but that everywhere I went I was surrounded by policemen. My behaviour was not very gracious; nor was it very popular with the officials responsible for me. Still, later in the evening I *was* able to talk freely with ordinary people.

The next day I took a sampan to cross one of the streams in Can Tho to reach the house of a rich peasant, Mr Dzu, I had visited in 1981. Alas, he had died a few months

Cyclos waiting for fares at Can Tho wharf

previously, but his wife would be happy to see me, I was told. She was. She fed her pigs and then her fish for me. As the meal was scattered on the water, vast catfish thrust themselves up, their ugly snouts and long antennae poking out of the water like sci-fi monsters.

Now I met also one of Madame Dzu's neighbours, Mr Anh, who was very pleasant. He and his daughter loaded their sampan with fruit and vegetables so that, for my benefit, we could go by boat to the market. At the market, a splendid covered affair on which boats were constantly converging to unload huge baskets of garlic, bananas or beans, Mr Anh made a great point of telling me that he always sold through the state – never in the private stalls with which the market also abounded. (After the Communist victory the government tried at first to suppress the private market, but recently, recognising its efficiency, it has been encouraging it once more.) Later, however, when the officials had departed, I saw the cunning Mr Anh just along the wharf – he had kept some of his produce from the state and was selling it privately for a better price than the state would give.

That evening I was sitting alone again in one of the little cafés, listening, I think, to Abba, when a young man in his twenties came tentatively up to me and asked, 'Are you English journalist?'

'Yes,' I said.

He replied, 'I think I remember you.'

I remembered him, too. I had met him here in 1981 and he had told me that his father had been in the navy in the old days, during the anti-Communist regime of President Thieu, which is now known officially as the puppet regime, and since 1975 they had been in a re-education camp. About 200,000 people, maybe more, no one knows, have been 're-educated' since 1975. None of them was tried; they were all simply incarcerated, with no idea of how long they would be inside or if and when they might be released. This boy had not seen his parents for years.

Off we went again the next day towards Cambodia – by road this time. I was told that the road here was so good that no one travelled by boat on the river. This did not seem likely – there were dozens of passenger-boats coming in and out of the Can Tho port every hour – but I accepted the analysis. It was a perpetual problem – first to find real boats taking real people to real places, and then to get myself allowed on them.

Outside the town the road was covered with great patches of gold – unhusked rice drying in the sun. Sampans were carrying it in great green bundles through the flooded fields to the roadside; there threshing machines were throwing the stalks in great fountains into the air and poorly dressed farmers, men and women, were raking the grains on the tarmac. The wealth of Vietnam was lying on that road – the only dry place. I wondered how much of it was lost as a result of trucks and buses ploughing through it every few minutes.

In Chau Doc, the last large town before the Cambodian border, we went, as usual, to the People's Committee Building, a fine old house on the river-bank. Here we were supposed to have lunch; and for once we were hungry at midday. The Vice-Chairman Responsible for Culture and Information, Comrade Tran Tuan, informed us that they had provided tea and oranges but no lunch. I said that we needed food but he was not to worry – we would go to a private restaurant in the town.

This led to a great debate – Party officials never seemed to like their guests to eat privately – and eventually, together with about ten local officials, we all piled into cars and were taken to a state restaurant. Upstairs we went and there were two tables, each set for six to eight people and with some food already on them. A bit rum, I thought, as we sat down.... And then the feast began.

Never in Vietnam have I seen such food. Not even in the days of the puppet regime. Certainly not since the triumph of Marxist Leninism. In the old days I saw food more delicately served, perhaps. But I never saw such delicacies as these served at all.

First there was tiger snake – *ran ho*. Then there were the air-bags of fish - *suu*. After that came some relatively ordinary dishes, chicken, both curried and roast, vegetables, meat and other fish dishes – I forget just how many – and all through there were masses of beer and vodka ('Vietnamese gasoline', as Comrade Long loved to call it). And finally there was the *pièce de résistance*. Onto each table was set a large plate containing three whole turtles. There they were, the entire creatures, little paws and tails poking out from under the shells, heads mercifully retracted.

One of the officials at my table was Comrade Huynh Van Nam, the Vice-Chairman of the Provincial Committee Responsible for the Distribution of Foodstuffs. 'How very appropriate that you should be here,' I said, which Tuc probably translated as, 'The Englishman is very fond of the warm weather in Vietnam.' He it was who now took the lids off the turtles to reveal inside ... *everything*. Full dorsal was the view we had. The entire turtles' workings. Tubes and pipes, bellows and liver, kidneys and muscles. And worst of all, perhaps, many little turtle eggs.

I regret to say that I found the animals hard to look at, and Tuc was also looking a little white. 'I have never eaten this,' she said. But there was no holding her southern comrades. With the speed of summer lightning their chopsticks began to dance and prance over the boiled turtles' bodies, picking and sawing away at the delicacies. There was one man who was especially adept – an impish man with a pleasing face. Not for a second did he falter; time after time his chopsticks left his mouth to make unerringly for a morsel which looked appalling to me but which I was assured by the looks of fury on the faces of the other comrades was choice indeed. I thought he must be a very important official, and was delighted to discover that he was one of the local drivers.

'A special toast to you, comrade driver,' I said, raising my small glass of Vietnamese gasoline and draining it in one.

Gradually more and more of the turtles' parts disappeared. I tried one piece very gingerly myself, and found that it tasted like salt rubber. I was offered eggs and politely declined them. In the end the only thing that was left was one tail.

'The tail is an aphrodisiac,' one official told me.

'Then how come no one has eaten it?' I asked.

'You have it,' said the Vice-Chairman.

'No, thank you,' I said. 'I am far from home. Comrade Chairman, you should have it.'

And so he did. He picked the thing apart in his chopsticks, plunged it into his mouth and took a large draught of beer. 'Tonight I sleep with my wife,' he said, and belched.

At about two o'clock, lunch was ended. I thanked our hosts and said how fine it was to see the people of Vietnam eat so well. Later I learned that they presented us with a bill for 6000 dong for the meal. Now at the official rate of exchange that is US $600, which seemed to me to be a little high even for such a repast. The whole incident made me laugh and laugh. What a brilliant sting! Every district has a budget for entertaining foreigners – usually, of course, Soviets and their ilk. We were arriving officially, and so this gave the Party the right to order a fine meal which they themselves would share – all on the budget. When we arrived they tried to palm us off with oranges and tea in the hope that they could have the feast entirely for themselves. When it became clear that this was impossible (only because we happened to be hungry; often we were quite happy with fruit for lunch) they gave in with reasonably good grace, but then insisted we pay. After a good deal of discussion among our guides, the bill was reduced to 3000 dong, or $300 at the official rate of exchange. But it represented only $30 at the rate at which most dollars are exchanged for bundles of old dong wrapped in grubby newspaper on the black market in Vietnam. A very cheap meal indeed, though who would actually benefit from the money, I had no idea – an official mistress, perhaps.

From Chau Doc a narrow causeway leads to Tanchau, which really is the last town on the Mekong before Cambodia. Houses are built in amongst the trees all along the causeway. On one side of it is a canal and on the other, at this time of year, the monsoon-swollen Mekong has burst over hundreds of thousands of acres of fields. So the causeway appears to be leading across a vast lake, the only dry land for miles around. It is very spectacular. Many of the people who live along it are Chams – Muslims.

   Tuc and I took an old sampan to run part of the way up the canal to Tanchau. It had been virtually commandeered by our local escorts, thus wrecking its owner's afternoon. I supposed that afterwards he would be subjected to long questioning as to what he and 'the foreigner' did or did not say to each other and how many crumpled dong changed hands. Back on shore a bizarre incident took place.

A floating home at Chau Doc

A boy by his family home at Tanchau

Our escorts did not much want us to film here; they kept insisting that we must move on to Tanchau where 'important officials' were awaiting us. As everywhere, we were surrounded by hundreds of children. And, as everywhere, our travelling companions tried to disperse them. They did not succeed. Worse than that, the children began to taunt and abuse them. Now there are many things that policemen do not like, and being mocked by children is one of them. The children became more and more shrill and contemptuous and finally, in fury, one of our escorts went to the truck and pulled out an air rifle. With this gun he then proceeded to threaten the children. Of course he had no intention of shooting anyone, but it seemed extraordinary that officials thought this an appropriate way to exert their influence.

We then proceeded slowly up the road. It was about 5 p.m. and nearly dark, and at one lovely turn in the road we stopped to watch the sunset. At this one of our escorts became very agitated.

'It's getting dark,' he cried – a fact which was obvious to us all. 'We must move on fast at once.'

It was clear that he was rather scared at being caught among the people after nightfall. When we got to Tanchau we found that the Party headquarters was heavily fortified and guarded.

The hotel at Tanchau was not the finest hotel I have stayed in. Perhaps it was not the worst, but there are many which I have – fortunately – forgotten. There were no lights, but there was a lot of mud on the floors and a lot of dirt in the rooms. There was one lavatory for the entire establishment, which apparently doubled as a brothel. This lavatory showed signs of overuse. Next morning, I was glad to get up to leave at 5 a.m.

Traders in a village near the Vietnam–Cambodia border

After more discussions as to whether we could go on a real boat with real people, or had to go on a Party launch, we were eventually allowed onto a real boat for a few miles. So we were off – on our last leg towards Cambodia. There had been a tremendous storm that night: the river was in fantastic flood as it rushed and gushed past us, and we made very slow progress upstream. We stopped at the last village before the border, and I sat in a litle café where hundreds of children gathered around laughing and shouting.

'*Lien So* (Soviet),' they said.

'*Kung fai Lien So* (I am not a Soviet),' I replied, to their apparent delight.

I had in my bag two hats – one with a sea-gull and one with a parrot swaying on top – which I now produced, and the children and I had a lot of fun. . . . Then it was on to the frontier.

The border was deserted; it was not used very much and was just a little hut in an open field on the flat bank. In it sat some immigration officers, but they had little to do, for there are not many travellers here. Cambodians and Vietnamese from the villages on each side of the border are allowed to travel freely back and forth in their sampans. The arrival of the BBC was quite an event, even if, after only a short while, we had to set off downstream again – destined for the airport at Ho Chi Minh City.

But that night en route we had a sudden and totally unexpected call from our other redoubtable guide from Hanoi TV, Mr Hong. He had gone on to Phnom Penh to try and induce the Cambodians to let us cross the closed border by boat. He had succeeded! he shouted. He had arrived in Tanchau just after we had left! We must return at once! And so, after a few hours' sleep, we did.

There on the river-bank at Tanchau was an old wooden boat with the Cambodian flag – yellow towers of Angkor on a bright-red background – fluttering in the wind. What a pleasure it was to see! Our friend Hong was wearing what looked like army fatigues, so that I did not recognise him at first. He had brought with him from the Cambodian Foreign Ministry two Cambodians whom I knew, Pich Savoun and Kim Tith – the latter had been my guide in 1981. Both of them were quiet, courteous and gentle, quite different from so many of the Vietnamese police with whom we had been dealing. I was so pleased to see them, and in great good spirits we piled aboard, along with Tuc and Hong who were coming with us to Phnom Penh.

At the Vietnamese customs post Mr Hong wore a People's Army of Vietnam cap. 'I am a colonel,' he joked. Maybe it was true – perhaps he was indeed a serving army officer as well as a guide. By now the flag on the boat had been changed: we were no longer flying the Angkor towers, but the Vietnamese yellow star. What was this boat? I wondered. Were the soldiers aboard Vietnamese or Khmer? At what level of illusion were we operating? Where is the truth in Indochina? Can foreigners ever really find it?

'Cambodia,' I said as I stepped ashore again a few hundred yards further upstream. 'Cambodia,' I repeated, grinning inanely from exhilaration. The immigration people were delightful, as delightful as I like to think only Cambodians can be, and then I walked into the little village, found a café which served Vietnamese beer, and told the crew. There in Maxim's-sur-le-Mekong we spent an hour of very good cheer. Then we set off again up the wide river. By now the Cambodian flag had been raised again.

Sitting on the cabin top Kim Tith told me, as I supposed he was bound to tell me, that I would find things much improved in Cambodia since my last visit two and a half years ago. 'There is now a Khmer-Soviet technical school,' he said. I asked him about food. Sadly he said that this year the monsoon was very late. The rice-fields were very dry and the harvest might be very badly affected.

We ran into an afternoon storm. Up ahead the clouds were black, and there was a dark line on the water before us. On the far side the water was flat, beaten down by rain, and the air above it was so full of rain as to appear like fog. On our side the water was still ruffled, the air above it clear. Then suddenly we were in it. The crew hastily lifted the old wooden shutters and on the bridge the doors were closed against the onslaught which came like a slap on the face.

Further upstream we passed two sunken ships, freighters which had been destroyed during the vicious 1970–5 war. Then the anti-Communist government of General Lon Nol in Phnom Penh had been besieged by the Cambodian Communists, the Khmer Rouge. Year by year, the Khmer Rouge had tightened their hold on the countryside and closed upon the capital. The Mekong remained the only lifeline, but then the Khmer Rouge seized its banks and rocketed and mined the ships bringing supplies up from South Vietnam. Ships were sunk, the convoys ended, and Phnom Penh fell. Now the masts and superstructures protruded from the water, ghostly relics of a war which was lost and which led to a retribution by the victors so terrible that no one could have envisaged it.

In the dark we landed at Neak Luong, a town which was accidentally bombed by B52s in 1973. The Foreign Ministry had sent two cars to pick us up and drive us on to Phnom Penh.

William Shawcross relaxes outside a waterfront café on the Mekong Delta

An ancient ferry leaves Phnom Penh for Kompong Chhnang

Above: melons about to be loaded on the ferry at Phnom Penh. Right: a stilt house on the Tonle Sap River

98

Above: a Kampuchean soldier in the grounds of Angkor Wat. Previous page: an aerial view of Angkor Wat

Above and overleaf: hill people at Chiang Khong, a village in Thailand

For over two hours we juddered along the wretched potholed road to Phnom Penh. There was little other traffic – just an occasional truck, or a bicycle without lights. We passed a few villages in which people were sitting around fires in front of their houses. Behind, the great Cambodian sugar-palm trees swayed against the dark sky, which was occasionally stabbed by lightning.

In the sixties Phnom Penh was one of the most exquisite towns in Asia, with fine, white and yellow-ochre buildings, charming squares and cafés which lent it a French provincial charm. Then during the seventies it had been overwhelmed first by refugees fleeing the fighting, the widespread bombing by B52s and other American, South Vietnamese and Cambodian aircraft, and then by the growing cruelty of the Khmer Rouge forces. After they captured Phnom Penh in April 1975 they closed the country off and embarked upon a ferocious revolution. The entire population of the city was forced at gunpoint into the countryside and spent the next three years in forced labour in an extraordinary, brutal agricultural gulag. The Khmer Rouge also embarked upon a war with their former allies, the Vietnamese, and as a result Vietnam invaded the country at the end of 1978. Then Hanoi set up its own version of a puppet regime, had shown to the world a prison in which the Khmer Rouge tortured and killed some of their victims and mass graves into which they had cast thousands more, and had sought international recognition. This had not been granted, and in 1983 the Khmer Rouge still held Cambodia's UN seat and war was still being waged between the Vietnamese troops in Cambodia and Khmer Rouge forces which were based along the border with Thailand. It is a dismal story.

The outskirts of the town were dark as we drove through them; most of Phnom Penh was still without electricity. The Hotel Monorom stood as a beacon of light. When we arrived there was no sign of Mme Sophan, the manageress, or her husband who had, with great skill and charm, transformed a wrecked shell into one of the most delightful and friendly hotels in Asia. Someone went up to fetch them. Her husband came down first.

We greeted each other warmly.

He went up to tell his wife and a few minutes later she came down, all smiles. 'I was not expecting you,' she said.

Curfew was at nine, so we left our gear in the hall and went to the restaurant down the road for a marvellous meal which included my favourite Cambodian soup – orange, tomato, fish and much else besides. As we left the restaurant a Cambodian came up to me in the street and whispered, 'Please write the truth about what you discover here.' I replied that I would try, and hoped that he would help me. He squeezed my hand and walked away. I went back to the Monorom. It's absurd, because I have spent so little time in Cambodia, but it felt almost like coming home.

The next morning I wandered around the streets of the city. Wrecked cars were piled on side-streets, and rubbish lay about in festering, uncollected heaps. There were armed Vietnamese troops outside the bank and other key buildings, and Cambodian militiamen lounged around or could be glimpsed lurking on top of trucks with their guns. Behind the hotel was a busy food market, ankle-deep in mud, bursting with Cambodian laughter and a gaiety which seems able to withstand almost anything. Nonetheless, just as when I was here two and a half years before, everything seemed to me tenuous, as if people were still so uncertain of the future that they were only camping, not settling. After the destruction caused by the war, the annihilation of the Khmer Rouge years, and the stagnation of Vietnamese occupation, the country has no industry and almost no infrastructure. The two hotels in town are just about the only official source of foreign exchange which the government enjoys.

I had never met any Cambodian who sought a return of the Khmer Rouge; nor did I this time. But there was, it seemed to me, growing impatience, on the part even of government officials, with the Vietnamese. Cambodian officials made it very clear to me that they resented the fact that we had come with Vietnamese guides. One old Cambodian friend said, 'More and more people are leaving. The liberators are becoming the colonisers. There are thousands of Vietnamese here now, everywhere. They have been settled in every quarter of Phnom Penh. They have much greater civil rights than we do. In the ministries they used to be called advisers. Now they are administrators. They run everything, make all the decisions. People leave for that reason.'

We had a long morning of negotiations in my room about what we could and could not do. The Cambodians sat silently as my Vietnamese comrades did a lot of talking. The Vietnamese asked us to promise not to tell anyone which day we planned to travel to Angkor Wat. 'There may be Khmer Rouge in the town,' they said, 'and if they hear of our movements they may attack us.' To the Vietnamese, no Cambodian could be completely trusted, it seemed.

In the afternoon I went on a tour of the town by cyclo. In the gorgeous gilded royal palace, which miraculously survived the war and revolution, people were filing through the sumptuous apartments and pausing to kneel before the emerald Buddha; it was an attractive Sunday scene. Across the courtyard floated the sounds of a Schubert sonata; in the music school a boy was practising the piano.

Then I was pedalled through the rain to Tuol Sleng, the prison in which the Khmer Rouge tortured and killed about 16,000 people. It's a horrifying place. On the walls of the rooms are the photographs of the victims before and after death. Some were children. If their parents were murdered here, then they were murdered too. The Vietnamese have tried to present the place as an 'Asian Auschwitz' – in fact it is much more like an Asian Lubyanka. Members of the Party and their families were killed here, after fantastic confessions were extorted from them. The Khmer Rouge were altogether more Stalinist than Nazi, but now I learned that the place is being remodelled – after the image of Sachsenhausen, which Cambodian officials had been sent to study. It seems to me that the intention of Vietnamese propaganda is to draw attention away from the fact that, like the regime in Hanoi, the Khmer Rouge were Marxist Leninists, and that, if anything, their crimes sprang from that creed, not from fascism.

I was allowed to take a passenger-boat – the passenger-steamer from Phnom Penh to Angkor Wat – for the next stage of my trip. What a journey! The boat was going all the way up the principal tributary of the Mekong, the Tonle Sap, to the Great Lake, the heart of Cambodia, then to Battambang, Cambodia's second city, and finally to the temples of Angkor itself. Two nights and two days. It was a pity that I was not allowed to go all the way on the boat – 'reasons of security', and 'pirates on the lake' were the explanations given – but it was wonderful to be able to travel on such a vessel at all. The harbour I already knew. The night before I had been to a delightful restaurant there, whose house speciality, I was told, was *Soupe de Poulet Rire* – 'Laughing Chicken Soup', which was chicken boiled with marijuana. I had ordered it, and all night long the soup enhanced my dreams – superbly.

The boat's name was *Sun and Moon*; she was a double-decked vessel, unlike all those I travelled on in Vietnam. Both decks were strung with scores of hammocks which the travellers had put up to live in and around for the next forty-eight hours. Mothers were suckling babies. Despite the 'security' problems, how easy and relaxed it all seemed compared with the business of boarding a real boat in Vietnam. When we set off from the Phnom Penh wharf and started to steam past the little bamboo huts which cover the bank, I was in high spirits. Some of the laughing chicken was still with me. Many of the people aboard were fishermen and their wives and children from the Great Lake. They had travelled down from Battambang or Siem Reap, near Angkor, with dried fish to sell in the markets in Phnom Penh. It is a far safer route than either the pock-marked roads or the train from Battambang – both of which the Khmer Rouge frequently ambushed. I talked to several fishermen. During the Khmer Rouge period of power some of them had been forced to leave their villages and work in the fields instead of fishing. They were all greatly relieved by the Vietnamese invasion of 1979, though by now there were mutterings that Vietnamese fishermen were taking too much of the fish for themselves and for Vietnam.

The captain of the boat was a delightful man in his late forties. During the Khmer Rouge period he too had been forced to work in the fields. He had concealed his identity – even a captain could be marked down as a 'bourgeois element' and would have risked execution. The boat itself had been beached; no such travel as people were now enjoying was then allowed. He invited me to join him on the bridge for an excellent lunch of rice and crab. I was very sorry when it was time to go ashore again.

The next day I took an open fishing-boat to a village at the bottom end of the Lake. Behind me came a large launch carrying an armed escort to protect me from pirates, or, I suppose, from possible Khmer Rouge attacks. The village was a poor place. It had barely any concrete structures, and most of the bamboo huts had nothing in them. There was little to buy in the market, and the children had the pot-bellies of malnutrition. Here too people said that during the Khmer Rouge time they had had to leave their homes; they had been forced into the nearby hills to break stones and collect wood. They were glad to be back. After talking with them, I had to drive back to Phnom Penh; along the roadside were the carcasses of tanks and armoured cars destroyed and abandoned in the all-too-recent wars.

Henri Mouhot, the French naturalist and explorer who rediscovered Angkor in the mid-nineteenth century, made his way right up the Lake – through bands of pirates, no doubt – to Siem Reap in search of the temples which had disappeared for centuries, literally swallowed by the jungle. My day-trip there was more prosaic but also exhausting, at least to me – in an ancient Russian helicopter of the Vietnamese army. (My Vietnamese guides had insisted that it was too dangerous to travel by road.) I don't much like helicopters at the best of times – when the one in which I

William Shawcross with his armed escort

have to travel originated in the USSR and has since done twenty years' war work in South-East Asia my dislike increases to pathological fear. Nonetheless, I forced myself aboard, comforted to see that travelling with us on the outing were the wife and children of a senior official of the Foreign Ministry. Then it must be all right, I thought.

We flew up the river and over the vast expanse of the Great Lake, the submerged trees peering out of it. I tried to spot the good ship *Sun and Moon*, but I suppose she had passed on before. After landing in Siem Reap we were rushed around only two of the great sites, Angkor Wat itself and the Bayon. This last is surrounded by woods within which there were said to be Khmer Rouge; we were guarded by more than 300 troops, according to our guides.

Our whole visit was so hectic – we were not permitted to stay the night: 'security' again – that I am ashamed to say that I found it hard at first to have any real feel of Angkor. But gradually, walking around Angkor Wat on my own, the grandeur of the place made me agree with Mouhot that the sight made the traveller 'forget all the fatigues of the journey, filling him with admiration and delight, such as would be experienced in finding a verdant oasis in the sandy desert'. Mouhot also felt that the temples transported the traveller, 'as if by enchantment ... from barbarism to civilisation, from profound darkness to light'. Remembering that Angkor had been founded and built upon an empire of slavery not totally dissimilar to that of the Khmer Rouge, I found the place more sinister than that – and the troops, one side of Cambodia's war, who surrounded us added to that feeling. But it was abidingly impressive nonetheless, and I was disappointed when my guides made it clear that it was time to return to the helicopter and Phnom Penh.

Back in the capital, I went to see the Lao Ambassador to ask whether it was going to be possible for me to continue my journey on the Mekong in Laos. With great courtesy he made it clear that the Vietnamese lobbying had failed; it was 'not convenient' for me to go to Laos at this time. The fabulous gorges through which the Mekong passes in northern Laos, on its journey between Tibet and the sea, would not be part of my journey.

And so I had to fly back from Phnom Penh to Ho Chi Minh City. I was sad to be leaving Cambodia; its travails are still so acute and there still seems to be no resolution of them anywhere in sight. 'What will happen to us?' one Cambodian friend asked me. 'What does the world think? Will there be another war? We are very frightened of another war.'

I could not reassure him.

In Ho Chi Minh City I was, as always, captivated by the warmth of ordinary Vietnamese. To my delight I was told that my friend who had threatened to leave by boat had not done so and was alive and well, though she still hoped to leave Vietnam. With real regret I said goodbye to Tuc and Hong; they had been superb guides, dealing on the whole very patiently with my prejudices. I left for Thailand on the same weekly Air France flight which had brought me in so long ago.

This must be the most poignant flight in the world; it is filled with Vietnamese refugees who have managed to bribe their way through the bureaucracy and exit legally rather than by boat. At the airport they are subjected to a final humiliation by officials as their bags and sometimes their bodies are searched to see what they are taking with them. In the plane they sit silently, apparently unable to believe that they are actually about to leave. Sometimes when the jumbo lifts off the tarmac there is a cheer, at other times gasps and sobs. The day I took the flight there was just the silence of exhaustion through the cabin as we lifted up over the Mekong and turned towards the west.

My next glimpse of the river was several hundred miles to the north-west where it winds out of Laos and forms the border between that country and northern Thailand. It was pouring with rain when I arrived in the little Thai town of Chiang Khong. It was not coming down like stair-rods, as someone said of it in Can Tho. But it had begun at around 2 a.m. the night before, pounding hard on the tin roof and the wood walls of the little Hotel Wathana, and by morning it was still there, draining out of a sky dull as dishwater, with no life, no light in it at all.

I sat on the balcony of the Hotel Wathana, drinking coffee, assaulting my typewriter and waiting for Amnat, a young boatman I had found, to arrive with a roar in his crazy, long-tailed speedboat to take me on the last leg of my journey up the river between Thailand and Laos to the Golden Triangle.

I had missed so much of the Mekong. Coming north from Cambodia after impassable falls in southern Laos, the river then curls west towards Thailand, and for several hundred miles it is the frontier between Thailand and Laos. For little mountainous Laos it is also the main highway from the capital, Vientiane, to the south. Just above Vientiane is the site of what would be one of the world's biggest dams if the United Nations Mekong Development Committee was ever able to bypass the political strife of the region and harness the waters for the whole area. From just above Vientiane the river leaves Thailand and disappears into the mountains of northern Laos up to the old royal capital of Luang Prabang. Then, turning west again through fierce and desolate hills, it comes back to Thailand just south of where I was now. From here it is again a border, first between Thailand and Laos, and then for one brief, glorious moment Burma, Laos and Thailand all meet together on the Mekong. This spot, known in Thailand as the Golden Triangle, is actually within the much larger, drug-producing area which all over the world is also known as the Golden Triangle. After that, the great river shades away again to China – which to my surprise is only about 40 miles from the Golden Triangle – and twists back to its birthplace in the Himalayas.

Chiang Khong was a lovely little one-street town, and in the shops below, saffron-robed monks, some just boys, were collecting their alms – their breakfast – from the townspeople, while dark-clothed hill tribespeople with silver bangles and large baskets and babies on their backs peered at the videos for sale. Even in such a tiny, relatively poor place there were almost 100 video machines. The contrast with Cambodia or Vietnam was extraordinary.

On the bank opposite was the equally pretty Lao town of Ban Houei Sai. Before the Communists won Laos, this used to be a busy border crossing, for smuggling as well as for people, but it is closed now. Still, since 1975 thousands of Lao refugees have crossed the Mekong, here and elsewhere, into Thailand; for them the river has been a bridge, not a barrier.

Amnat arrived before nine, together with friends, including a drunken driver. I invited them to breakfast but all they wanted was Thai Mekong whisky. Fair enough, I said; it was cold and they had been on the river since dawn. But as far as the driver was concerned it was a mistake, as I found as soon as we set off.

The speedboat was about 20 feet long, had no draught at all and was powered by a Datsun car engine mounted on the stern. Its speed was extraordinary even against the power of the Mekong, which was narrower and faster here than I had seen it anywhere on the journey. By the same token, the boat was not very stable – particularly in the hands of the dipsomaniac driver.

There were no seats on the boat; I squatted on the floor and the driver let out the clutch with such a bang that I practically fell into the propeller shaft. Then he put the helm hard to port, so hard that the boat skidded wildly and almost overturned. Once we got going, we travelled so fast over the surface of the water that I could scarcely breathe for the slipstream. The engine was so loud I could not speak at all. It was, to be precise, exciting.

A brace of duck wheeled up out of the rushes of Thailand as we roared by, glided across the river and, knowing no borders, settled in Laos. The mountains here come

William Shawcross in the long-tailed speedboat en route to the Golden Triangle

down to sip at the river, their heads cosseted still in cloud. The water was boiling, rolling, white, rocks passing us at 30 miles an hour, the driver struggling to hold us steady, failing. At one point the Thai flag on a stick above the engine caught fire. The driver tore it off and flung it into the bilge which was swimming in petrol. Fortunately there was a lot of water there too. A little further on the engine began to scream – the prop had sheared. The driver couldn't change it – his hands were shaking too much. At last my childhood sailing memories came in useful.

It was at the end of this day that I reached the end of the journey: a little bamboo shack on the water's edge. The Golden Hut it was called, and golden it remains in my memory. A tiny inn at the apex of Thailand, 2 feet from the river, Burma 20 yards to my left across a tributary, Laos half a mile across the main river to my right. I sat with a Thai beer and thought what a wonderful day it had been; what fun, what a rolling, rollicking day. The roar of the engine was still jiggling the marrow of my bones, ta-ta-ta-ing on my ear-drums, and I could think only of the speed of the boat, the bubbling of the water, the lowering of the mountains, the swaying of the hills, the coming of the plains again with the mountains higher but further back from the water, the mingling of the mists in the forests, and the afternoon sun finally breaking through to glimmer on the water and to steam on the damp trees and the dark mountains stretching into China, and an evening rainbow joining Laos to Burma.

I had supper with Amnat on the floor of the Golden Hut, by a little fire on the riverside. A young man came by with a bamboo hookah. He filled it with Mekong water, began to cut up some leaves, and suggested that I join him for a smoke. The roar of the engine receded and the marrow settled down.

I walked up to the temple on top of the hill behind me and gazed for a long time at the different greys below which were Burma, the river, Laos and Thailand. An island midstream appeared as a thin black smudge in the river and seemed in the dark to resemble a battleship – from China, or from the USSR, or from somewhere else.

It reminded me in this peaceful place of the wars and the suffering that were being endured on the Mekong further south. Back at the hut, I lay on the bamboo bed just by the water. Here the Mekong was still, but out in midstream the torrent was rushing past me and on through Laos, through Cambodia and down to Bentre in the Delta where even now, for sure, boat people were trying to take the night tide out to sea, away from Comrade Long and his white-shirted lieutenants, away from their despair to a very uncertain future. From where I lay, the river sounded so soft for such a flood – rustling not hustling, a dim breaking of occasional waves on a distant shore. As I listened, I thought how terribly lucky, how extraordinarily privileged I was.

Two young monks at the Golden Triangle

THE SÃO FRANCISCO

Germaine Greer

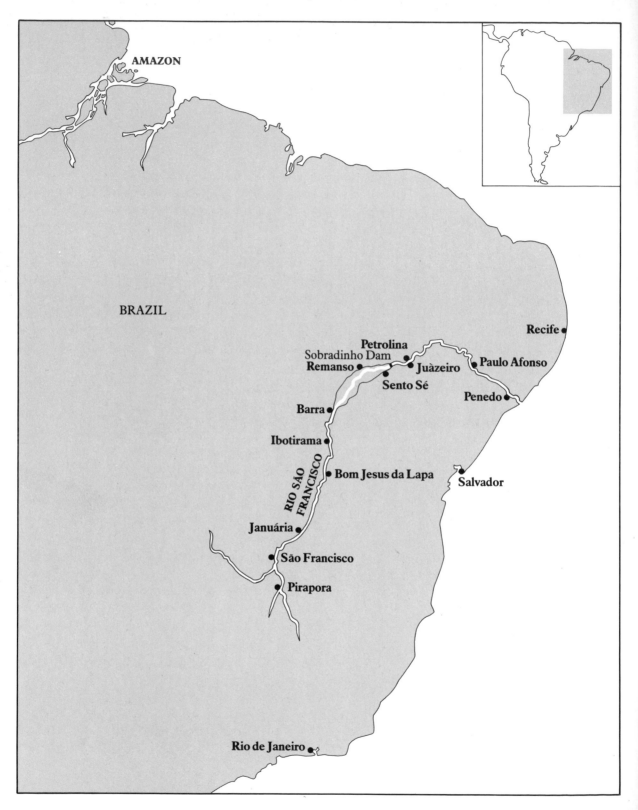

AMAZON

BRAZIL

Recife

Petrolina
Sobradinho Dam
Remanso
Juàzeiro
Paulo Afonso
Sento Sé
Penedo
Barra

Ibotirama

RIO SÃO FRANCISCO
Bom Jesus da Lapa
Salvador

Januária

São Francisco

Pirapora

Rio de Janeiro

An old man is selling honey in the market at Juàzeiro. It is wild honey that he has collected in the *caatinga*, the dry scrubland that takes over beyond the narrow alluvial strip along the river São Francisco. The volatile oils given off by the tough little plants that grow there make the air of the *caatinga* as heady as wine, if a wine could be so hot and so thin. The flowers of the *caatinga* are either short-lived or tiny and sparse. The beehives are few and far between. The old man has put his treasure into litre bottles, which he has stopped with whittled wooden plugs round which the honey oozes in the heat, full of charred particles left from the murder of the bee community.

Stupidly I ask if he can sell me just half a litre. The old man, who, I should have realised, must have tramped in from the back blocks, lugging his six bottles that must have grown heavier with every step since the sun rose scorching from the instant that it showed above the horizon, had stood all day hoping to find someone to buy his elixir. He gazes wordlessly up at me and over his face steals a look I have come to know, a look which I was to see often in the valley of the Rio São Francisco. It contains elements of trust and of puzzlement, of scepticism and innocence, but although it questions or rather wonders, it demands no explanation. The old man's look told me that I was not aware of his dilemma, that I was not within hailing distance of the reality of life for poor farmers in the Nordeste, and he had no hope that I or any other person of my age, class and background ever would be, and that he did not resent it. There was no way that he, a poor farmer eking out a meagre subsistence on a *roça*, a small farm which would grow a little corn, beans and manioc if the rains were adequate, and nothing at all if they were not, could lay his hands on two half-litre bottles. God knows he had scavenged to find the litre bottles he already had. He said nothing but turned his head slightly and stared into the distance. Ashamed, I put down my 5000 cruzeiros and touched his sleeve. He did not smile as he folded up the bills and put them in the inside pocket of his tattered jacket. I carried that sticky bottle for thousands of miles before I gave it away.

Perhaps I would not have reacted in such a way if it had not been for the fact that my father died in Australia the day that I left England for Brazil. He had wanted no fuss and there was none, but the reality of the Nordeste scraped on a sensibility more than usually raw. I had first seen that look on my father's face. In fact, I had come to dread it, because it meant quite clearly that he was being overwhelmed. It was as if all the veils of social attitudinising and defensiveness had dissolved and for an awful moment I could see into his soul. Too often that look of lostness would give way to a terrible grimace of distress as out of the gathering darkness in his brain his old anxiety neurosis rose up and grabbed him. It is the look of humanity come to the last ditch, beyond help or the hope of help. You may see something very like it in the eyes of children and idiots, but it is not at all vacant or uncommunicative. Rather it speaks of pure humanity, beyond personality. Each time I saw it in the eyes of the people of the Rio São Francisco, it seemed to tell of the sadness of the human condition and the fatuity of our cherished notions of progress.

A little boy with parotitis is listening to his mother tell the missionary doctor how his father was sent home from the hospital to die of a cancer his family had known nothing about. The mother is giving her grief and shock their proper, dramatic expression, but the little boy's face is completely distorted because his cheek protrudes like the nose-cone of a rocket. Only his eyes tell the story. The look intensifies as the unqualified doctor prods his hard cheek and confidently declares the necessity of taking a tooth out. The child cannot know that he is wrong, but the eyes tell me that he has no expectation of his being right. The look persists as the doctor indulges in a sermon on the importance of not living in the past. (The child's father has been dead three days and there is no money for a decent burial.)

The neighbours told me that the little boy supported his family by fishing all day in the river with a hand-line. A good throwing net would have done more for the parotitis – and the look – than an unnecessary tooth extraction, but the wearers of the look both old and young know that official aid does not recognise their reality. Instead of giving him a throwing net, official aid would insist that the child go to school.

The people of the Nordeste of Brazil are descended from now-exterminated Indians, escaped slaves and European adventurers, in varying proportions. The result is a fantastic array of human types with extraordinary and exotic combinations of colouring and feature, living side by side even in the extremity of poverty. Smooth-faced girls with perfect Ethiopian features may have golden eyes and hair like curled golden wire. Others with night-black skin may have straight hair and grey eyes. A very few have the beautiful ruddy skin and tiny hands and feet of the vanished Indian tribes. Under the *vaqueiro*'s greasy leather hat, you may find a face as Irish as Macgillicuddy's Reeks, encrusted with skin cancers. This bewildering variety is orchestrated by the Nordestino smile, wide, spontaneous, uncalculating, shy and friendly at the same time. Other people are not yet an instrument for one's own ends in the Nordeste. Each meeting is a recognition of another person as unique and interesting as oneself, and the Nordestino smile expresses a mixture of surprise and delight not often met with at cocktail parties.

That smile is often to be seen in conjunction with the look. A beautiful man with skin as black and smooth as jet is smiling as he tells another doctor in another clinic how he fell while working on a water-tower for the town council. He has crawled and hopped into the room, clinging to any handhold he can find. In his face there is no mark to show that he is forty years old, father of nine children, with nothing to expect from life but pain and destitution. Occasionally he coughs a short, dry cough. His smile does not waver as the doctor tells him to drag himself somehow to the TB clinic miles away downriver. The smile is dazzling but the eyes are appalling.

Other people did not seem to see the look. I may have imagined it after all. Perhaps my own guilt about my neglect of my father's obsequies caused me to see the ghost of his look in so many places. It is embarrassing to admit that I think I saw it in the eyes of a funny-looking wading bird with a ragged topknot, and in the eyes of the small boy who had hoped so hard to sell it to the hotel menagerie in Pirapora.

Perhaps I was simply haunted and that might be why the Valle do Rio São Francisco seems to me to be the worst example of fake development and the modernisation of poverty that I have ever encountered. I was not so upset by Calcutta; even in the refugee camp there at Salt Lake in 1972, pity and despair were effectively held at bay. In the slums of Bombay or Bangkok or Port Sudan it seemed to me that the people had a future. Certain values adhered, certain structures cohered. The people, however scrambling and desperate, seemed to have a chance of surviving as themselves. The worst of Penedo, Juàzeiro, Bom Jesus da Lapa and Pirapora is paradise compared with these vast, pestiferous warrens, and yet I found it deeply depressing. It seems only proper to explain that I am not a camera and may have seen everything asquint.

An old woman from the Nordeste of Brazil with her two grandchildren

The São Francisco River rises in the well-watered state of Minas Gerais and flows northward. By the time it crosses into Bahia, springs and tributary streams have all but disappeared and for most of its 2660-kilometre length the river flows through the 'drought polygon' where the annual rainfall amounts to only 400 millimetres and the inhabitants may rely on 2800 hours of sunlight a year and an average temperature of twenty-five degrees centigrade. In these latitudes the sun passes close to the zenith and the thin, dry air can do little to blunt the burning edge of its steep rays. Sun-bathing along the São Francisco is a dangerous pastime; nevertheless you may see provincial ladies of leisure, well basted with smelly oils, grilling themselves by hotel swimming-pools in the burning middle of the day when everyone else has taken shelter. It is only a matter of time before someone decides to build a tourist complex on Sobradinho dam, but it will need its own burns unit.

The minute rainfall arrives in summer; in the winter the sparse forage for the scrawny cattle which are the chief industry of the *sertão* must be supplemented by cutting cactus which is actually cultivated, planted out in neat rows inside thickset hedges of thorn or *avellós*. The sandy, stony soil of the *sertão*, which contains no humus, cannot produce enough vegetation to support the cattle population at the density which 500 years of lordly ranching have imposed unless the *vaqueiro* serves the animals hand and foot. The meat yield is comparatively poor and there is no export market. The *vaqueiro* sees himself as a member of an élite, but he lives in a windowless mud house without sewerage or clean water and he eats manioc and goat's meat and he cannot read or write. His house and his land usually belong to his master, the *fazendeiro*. If an animal in his care breaks a leg he will be turned out. The *vaqueiro* is very much aware that the culture of the *sertão* is his culture, as he quaffs his *cachaça* and sings his improvised songs of flattery to his oppressors or tightens the bearing-rein and pulls his little horse's mouth to pieces in order to clatter past a group of onlookers with all his fringes flying. He is proud, charming, powerless and pathetic.

We happened upon the Valle do Rio São Francisco at a fortunate time, for the rains, such as they are, had just fallen. The desert was blooming in clumps of vivid flowers which had popped out of the stony earth like feathers out of the barrel of a toy gun. Within a week most of them had completed their life-span; their stems had crumbled into dust and their seed capsules had burst, leaving their cargo to lie dormant for another year, or more, if the rains should fail, as they often do. The air was so thin and clear that ridges 60 miles away stood out as if cut from the blanched sky. I and the BBC TV crew travelled, as do all those rich enough to travel at all in the Nordeste, in a small aircraft, skimming along the crystal air, hiccuping occasionally on the thermals. As Juàzeiro came in sight the air was thickening slightly with the approach of evening. The oblique light struck off the surface of the river in a thick, white band. Fifty kilometres upstream the band became a blaze which filled the whole horizon, Sobradinho, the largest man-made lake in the world.

Next to me on the plane sat an Italian wine-grower from Rio Grande do Sul, going to Santa Maria da Boa Vista to check on the progress of his new table-grape plantation. He was full of optimism, for none of the diseases that plague wine-growers in the south can flourish in the dry air of the *sertão*. By regulating the availability of water to the different sections of the plantation, it should be possible to ripen grapes in every week of the year. The valley of the São Francisco River could be a new California, a new Israel. If I had known more then I would have asked him why the government of the state of Pernambuco had approached an entrepreneur from the south in order to develop grape-growing, and how the deal had been set up and how many local people were employed on the project.

A neighbouring project, Bebedouro, developed by CODEVASF, the São Francisco Development Company, employs a small number of families, who are allowed to settle in the project area only after they have satisfied 'carefully established criteria: the admission requirements thus include a study of their past life, scholarship (primary school at least) and, finally, a trial period, during which production capacity, ability to learn agricultural techniques and behaviour in community will determine whether or not they are qualified for the project'. In return for displaying conspicuous fitness, the families are allowed to work long hours on intensive agriculture for the profit of others. They are tied to the land, living 'in comfort in small villages especially built for this purpose'. On the island of Cabrobó, which I later visited on my river journey, I saw such a small village, mud huts roofed with thatch, with no cleaner water and no better plumbing than anywhere else. Where the independent farmers could spend a good deal of time sitting dreaming before their house-door when the short growing season was over, the irrigation workers had to shoulder their mattocks every day, though the heat blistered. By the time I saw the captive 'Indians' of Cabrobó, for the people of Cabrobó are corralled even more securely in what passes for a reservation, I knew how to interpret the fact that almost all the irrigated crops I saw were salt-tolerant luxury items (as are table-grapes) destined for the tables of Rio and São Paulo at competitive prices. By the time I left Brazil, I had come to loathe watermelon as a symbol of useless frittering away of human resources, but that first afternoon on the plane slithering into the airport at Petrolina, I caught my companion's enthusiasm. The blinding glare of the huge dam on the southern horizon was the emblem of that new future.

As we drove in from Petrolina airport we passed houses made of the Nordestino version of wattle and daub, sun-dried red mud forced between closely planted wooden stakes. Come rain or high water it would simply wash out again. The houses, roofed in carnauba palm, were half hidden behind walls of the same closely planted wooden stakes that held up the mud walls, these exposed and bleached silver by the sun. Within the compound the red earth was swept clean of every turd, weed or stone, so that it could function as an extension to the tiny house. At the back you might see the cooking place, which was no more than three stones set in a triangle. The pot sat above and the firewood was fed in from the sides, burning frugally at the tips and carefully extinguished when the cooking was done. Already it was obvious that wood was both an essential commodity and in short supply. Before the house-door stood a shade tree, the only stout and permanent feature of the whole arrangement, and under it sat the inhabitants, peeling manioc or pounding grain or playing with their babies. In line with the open front door of the house stood a back door, likewise open, creating a draught which dried the sweat and cooled the skin of those sitting under the tree. The principle was simple and, I was to discover, very effective.

119

Women moved through the courtyards with the studied languor of those for whom energy conservation is a prime consideration. The gathered skirts of their washed-out print dresses often hung high in the front, pushed out by a pregnant belly. Around the houses stood fields of manioc and sugar-cane and a forage called *capin*.

Abruptly the fields ended, cut off by a chain-link fence stretching farther than the eye could see. Inside this vast enclosure, cheek by jowl, marching in formation up and down the low hills, was row upon row of identical semi-detached houses, each pair so minute that the façades had room only for the two doors and the two windows. Here was no shade tree, no yard space, but simply a hermetic box for living in, with no gap between wall and roof for cooler air to circulate. Electricity would provide climate control, even if cooking (with electricity) were to be done inside the house. Here were sewerage and clean water, but here was neither privacy nor individuality nor character. The rows of houselets were more like a military camp than a suburb, or some cheaper version of the slave housing built on plantations in South Carolina and Louisiana 200 years ago. Moreover, they appeared to be deserted.

I was to see these *casas popolares* in urban centres large and small all along the Rio São Francisco. In every case the construction was mean, the design stupidly regular and symmetrical, the allocation of space meagre. The idea of providing cheap permanent housing with power, sewerage and treated water, and establishing a Banco de Habitação which would finance mortgages and rental purchases, was a good one, but it was not working, not because the people rejected the official notion of what would be good for them, but because while the monthly payments rose in step with an inflation rate of the order of 120 per cent a year, employers evaded the government regulation which stipulated that wages be automatically adjusted by firing and rehiring their staffs at lower rates. Besides, qualifying for a *casa popolare* was rather like getting a job in a government irrigation scheme; only suitable types would be accepted.

The housing projects were terrible emblems of new forms and new norms of social control. In a society riddled with patronage and its inevitable concomitant, corruption, a provident man would do better informally than by becoming a pawn in a government scheme; the improvident man, whether sick, disabled or landless, was not eligible for inclusion in the scheme in the first place. The only person I met who lived in a government housing project held down three jobs and earned his monthly rental-purchase payment in a day. Money has been made out of the schemes by those who sold land, awarded contracts, supplied materials, subcontracted labour and distributed the units, but the pattern is the familiar one: a few made fortunes to add to the fortunes they already had, while the many lost. To the houseless hordes of Petrolina/Juàzeiro the myriad pitched rooflets which pinked the skyline might as well have belonged to houses on the moon.

Before breakfast next morning I took a car and went off into the pink heat shimmer to see where the people really did live. The nucleus of Juàzeiro is a grid of tight painted façades behind which chains of narrow rooms open one out of the other in a vista of glimmering tiled floors and a welter of gimcrack furniture bedizened with crocheted mats, doilies, antimacassars, coasters, runners, plastic flowers and gaudy images of popular cult figures: O Preto Velho, Padre Damiano (who foretold the bursting of the Sobradinho dam which is now rather overdue) and the Queen of the

Sea (who looks a lot like Hedy Lamarr). Nothing could have been more squeaky clean than these long wedges of house, crammed not only with pot plants and birdcages but with people of all sizes, mostly small. The noise level was unearthly, for not just every house, but every occupant of every room in every house, had a different idea of the exact kind of popular music that would make the day go with a swing. In order to be heard everybody screamed like a macaw. In case any chink of silence should remain to disfigure the perfect din, most houses kept a pair of green parrots with clipped wings that peeped out from their homes under refrigerators and gas cookers and shrieked until the sky rang.

There were no print dresses or bare feet to be seen here. The ampler, middle-class matrons of downtown Juàzeiro preferred to squeeze themselves into shiny lycra leotards as tight as sausage-skins. The nether quarters were carefully hidden in stiff new jeans, but the upper areas were in full view. Brown bosoms oozed round the strapless, one-strapped, frilled, shirred and altogether most inventively tarted-up and mostly fairly transparent leotards, so that the entire female population seemed to be on its way to an audition for *Fame*. The ensemble was completed by an elaborate, hieratic head-dress of coloured plastic curlers, over which the hair was pulled so tight that the skin at the temples was pleated. These fashions were to be observed all up and down the river, but it was some time before I managed to ask a young woman who had worn her curlers day in, day out for a week why she never removed them. When she did, the result was a rather ragged little pony-tail, which, as long as there was no kink in the tightly drawn-back hair, she found perfectly satisfactory. By evening the curlers had reappeared. Conventional wisdom had it that the women were trying to look European, but I persisted in thinking that the real aim was to look as Indian as possible. Certainly the few women whose hair did hang like blue-black silk were inordinately proud of it.

A street scene showing a woman wearing plastic hair-curlers

The car crashed from pothole to pothole, as the old cobbled roads gave way to sluices of sand in which it yawed and slewed and slid, the motor coughing as the carburettor breathed in more sand to add to what already swirled up and down the fuel line. The lycra glamour and commercial cacophony of the centre were soon left behind. The ruins of grandiose town-planning schemes lay all about. Grids of paved street stood up above the seas of sand, while the traffic wove itself through the breaks in the tumbledown ramparts. Broad carriageways led their rows of empty lamp-standards slap into blank walls. Scrawny cattle of mixed race, mostly zebu, picked their way daintily through the mess on their way to graze on the river-flats. A huge bus station with quays and platforms and shelters and even a snack-bar stood cut off from the roadway by a 10-foot drop. Up by the tarmac sat a small crowd of hopeful passengers under an improvised tarpaulin. Although their bundles of bedding and smoky cooking fires betokened a long stay they all gazed fixedly up the road as if a bus was due in five minutes.

Makeshift shelters began to proliferate. The driver was puzzled by my insistence that he plough farther and farther from the paved road, where there was no sign of regular streets and he had to navigate by following vague tyre-tracks in the sand. The people crammed into the tiny shanties stared out at us. Pigs rooted in the human excrement in the road. We passed files of women with kerosene tins of water on their heads. We saw other women too, sitting open-legged by the roadside, gazing expect-antly as we dragged our dust trail towards them. Even at a quarter to seven in the morning their demeanour was unmistakable. The Bishop of Juàzeiro was to tell me three times in a single conversation (and I myself had not brought up the subject) that there were 2000 prostitutes in Juàzeiro. If by prostitute he meant any woman struggling to live any way she can, including offering sexual services for money, the estimate was a conservative one. If he meant women actually making a living by prostitution, the estimate was fantastic. Juàzeiro was a town of would-be prostitutes without clients. The manners of the younger leotard-wearers in town were as free as those of their role models from the Avenida Paulista in São Paulo, which they studied continually on television and in the glossy gossip magazines. The men they rubbed up against under the trees along the river quays were the ones who might have brought a few cruzeiros to the desperate women in the mud huts out on the vast fringes of the city. Wherever the men in our film crew went, girls called out to them, ogled them, accosted them, hid amorous notes in their baggage. The men preened, correctly interpreting the lovesick chorus as a tribute to their conspicuous success in being rich, employed, healthy and white, and did nothing beyond a little mild show-ing off. For all the atmosphere of extravagant willingness, sex is still a serious matter in the Nordeste, if only because contraception in any form is practically unknown. First births occur early and most unions are informal, in the pattern familiar to us from other post-slavery societies. Some of the priests struggling against this sexual chaos refuse to baptise children unless their parents agree to marry at the same time. The threat is toothless because Nordestino religion is only partly based on Catholicism. Given the real magnitude of the problem, the humanitarian enterprise of the Diocese of Juàzeiro, which undertakes to teach 'prostitutes' needlework as a better way of making a living, is simply ludicrous.

We began our river journey at Juàzeiro in the middle of the river rather than at the source or the mouth because we had to rendezvous with our paddle-steamer for the journey upstream to Pirapora. The boat, the *São Francisco*, was the star of our show, and the film crew, understandably, were very keen to get to know her. From my hotel balcony I could see her yellow-painted funnel and her upper storey as she rode, or rather sat, at anchor beside the basalt-paved slipway, part of the elegant system of quays built in an earlier era, when the river carried goods and passengers and some of the wealth generated by sugar and leather percolated to the river towns. There was little or no activity on the river now. It flowed full, fast and turbid towards the rapids below Santa Maria da Boa Vista. I was not to learn for some time that this high level was artificially maintained, or that the exigencies of feeding the six hydroelectric stations 350 kilometres downstream at Paulo Afonso had caused devastating floods in Juàzeiro for three years in succession. The São Francisco had never been a sleepy, silty river, but a swift and sandy one. Fifty years ago when the *remeiros* poled their long boats down it, the voyage back upstream was a terrible ordeal, for they had to force the boats against the strong current by jamming the punt-pole hard against their breastbones until their chests were laid open. These fearful wounds were cauterised with boiling tallow in an agonising ritual.

The Paulo Afonso hydroelectric scheme

The *São Francisco* had begun life on the Missouri River in 1913; to ply the São Francisco she needed a special piece of equipment, a large anchor hanging from the prow. When her flat bottom ground to a halt on the shifting sand-bars of the 'Velho Chico', as the river was affectionately called, a sailor would wade out with the anchor, to which a winch-cable was attached, until he found deeper water. He would drop the anchor and the steamer would pull herself across the bar by winching in the cable. Apart from our boat, and another hulk rotting beside her, the only paddle-steamer doing business in Juàzeiro was working high and dry in one of the town squares as a restaurant. We had been told that there was a monthly boat carrying general passengers upstream and crossing another on the journey down, but, although the people who told us this appeared to believe it, and many citizens repeated the information, no such boats existed. When our paddle-steamer, or *gaiola*, came in sight of the river towns, she was the first they had seen in three years. What we eventually came to realise, as she panted and waddled ever more slowly, making a bare 5 or 6 knots and burning whole forests to make even that, was that she was also the last they would ever see. She had been refurbished to make a last voyage upriver, which is to say that the rust had been given a few coats of silver stove paint and the woodwork brightened up and the BBC had subsidised the cost of passage so that real people could travel with us. She seemed to me as trumpery as any stage set.

The stern wheel of the *São Francisco*

I was afraid that once we were borne away from the confusion and the squalor on the broad, cool river, sipping *caipirinhas* (wonderful drinks made with *cachaça*, whole limes and sugar) on her shaded upper deck, the reality of the Nordeste would slip beyond my grasp. Once the *São Francisco* arrived in Pirapora she would make short day-trips for the tourists staying at the hotel there, if indeed she would do so much. Despite frantic attempts to maximise the tourism potential of the valley of the São Francisco, and the determined exploitation of anything even faintly picturesque, the tourist industry has failed to take off.

Instead of visiting our star steamer, I prowled about Juàzeiro, trying to estimate how important the river was to the people. It was important to the cows daintily refraining from eating the fat curare plants on the river-flats. It was important to the women bashing clothes at the water's edge, and it was important to the children who splashed in the shallows beside them. The Diocese, mind you, seemed to think the women would be better off washing the clothes in a shed on the other side of town, where tubs and water (but not washing machines, despite the cheap hydroelectricity for which their town had been flooded) were provided.

Never have I encountered a population which did more washing than the Nordestinos, washing of heads and bodies, washing of plates, washing of clothes, washing of goats' entrails, washing of cars, washing of floors, even washing of walls. Some of the finest houses in Juàzeiro were covered all over with bathroom tiles, so that the outside could be as efficiently scoured and polished as the inside. The people without piped water to their houses washed in any water they could find, including the river. A man with nothing to his name but a pair of shorts would wash his shorts and wait in the water until the scorching sun had dried them. The importance of washing is not to be confused with an understanding of hygiene, for the Nordestinos would fish, wash and pee in the same river, as well as throw rubbish into it and drink from it. Decaying fragments of animal carcasses and human excrement fouled the alleyways where children played, and maggots teemed in the open drains.

Rather, washing seemed to have ritual importance. The Nordestino religion, called among other things *macumba* or *candomblé*, is a patchwork of voodoo, spiritism, animism and debased Catholicism, but the central ritual is cleansing. On the strange market stalls hung with leopards' paws and alligator skins, the array of soaps, washes, lotions, fumigant powders, douches and astringents, all mendaciously labelled as being concocted from plants of the African coast, gives evidence of religious observance principally composed of endless ablutions. Unofficial religion has got itself mixed up with unofficial medicine, and the same stalls sold herbal remedies based on European and Indian lore. Both the religion and the medicine existed for the same reason, because the people had no other resource. If every tattered cloth they owned and every battered tin dish was washed within an inch of its life, a sort of order was imposed on chaos. Even little children stood in the river and scrubbed their legs and their flip-flop sandals. Only when I saw a group of women struggling to wash in an encrusted puddle no larger than a tea-tray did I begin to understand the importance of washing to these people, and then more than ever I cursed the kind of development which brings electricity and the twaddling soap operas of TV Globo to the poor and will not, cannot, lay a water pipeline to save their babies' lives.

So, while the crew investigated the boat and gauged the level of its picturesqueness, I haunted the less salubrious purlieus of the city, peeping in at doorways where dozens of sweating people sat entranced by the soap operas 'Pane, Pane, Beijo, Beijo' or 'Louco Amor' in rooms not 10 feet square, peering through the gate at the exclusive country club, so exclusive indeed that it appeared to be derelict, always coming back to the market, where it seemed to me I could see athwart the economic reality of life in the interior. There was not much buying and selling going on. The vendors waited, and crowds of small boys waited by their wheelbarrows, hoping that some-one would pay them to push her purchases home. Occasionally a matron resplendent in leotard and curlers sailed by, with a barrow-boy in her wake, struggling to keep his barrow with its towering load of watermelons and yams from tipping its costly cargo into the maggoty muck underfoot. The sinews on their little arms stood out like bowstrings.

It would have been surprising if the Brazilian government and most of the func-tionaries we met had not assumed that we had come to Brazil to make a tourist film. Brazilians, even the poorest and most isolated, are intensely aware of the media. We had only to let our eyes, let alone the camera's eye, rest for an instant on any individual for him to start performing, even if all he was doing was washing his car or scratching his crotch. Everyone we met had his own idea of what we would want to see, and no scruple whatsoever in rigging it up whether we encouraged him or not, and then demanding a fee for doing it. When I began asking about infant mortality rates, or parasitic infestation, or the resurgence of malaria, or the unrestricted sale of dangerous drugs and baby foods or antibiotic abuse, everyone lost interest. As I was a woman, it was difficult for any Nordestino to imagine that what I thought about anything was of any interest to anybody. At times I despaired of ever putting together an intelligent film, and never more than in those early days in Juàzeiro. The chief cause of my misery was that ghastliest of all the ghastly manifestations of fake folk art, the *carranca*.

In the days when cargo-boats plied the river, some were decorated with grotesque figureheads, which no one found particularly remarkable. When the river trade lan-guished, the boats rotted and the figureheads rotted with them, until an enterprising collector realised that they were eminently collectable. In the time-honoured fashion of the art impresario he began a systematic study of them, pointing out correspon-dences (of a fairly inevitable kind) with figureheads from Phoenicia and medieval Turkey. Amidst all the brouhaha there emerges one *carranqueiro* of genius, Francisco Guarany, who began making *carrancas* in 1901 at the age of seventeen, and by 1940 had made about eighty of them. When the *carranca* cult developed he was persuaded to parody himself and made figureheads for boats which no longer existed. A tribe of *carranqueiros* who had never seen the genuine article began to produce thousands of *carrancas* which may be seen in every curio shop in Brazil, hideous perfunctory things made of unseasoned wood crudely lacquered in red, white and black and of all sizes, some tiny enough to fit on pencils, others huge. One, outside Juàzeiro, stands $3\frac{1}{2}$ metres tall. Almost all these objects are crude, soulless and utterly spurious; the common prejudice against the Nordestino people can only be reinforced by them.

The thought of being forced by circumstances to treat these objects seriously in

A *carranca* on the bridge of the *São Francisco*

our film produced in me a sensation not unlike panic. We were committed to struggle out into the *sertão* in the blinding heat in a VW Kombi, which boiled and threatened to leave us stranded on the blistering macadam at any moment, to pay homage to a *carranqueiro* called Xuri. His *carrancas* were only half a notch better than the usual rubbish, but still I was not sorry that we were there, or that the director of the film had commissioned a huge *carranca* (although I prayed that we would not actually have to show it in the finished film). The beautiful thing about Xuri was not his spurious craft activity but his whole life. He lived in a tiny house, with two tiny rooms and one larger one with door fore and aft. The whitewashed adobe was velvety cool to the touch, and the mild draught through the tiles and the gaps between walls and roof kept the air fresh. In a miniature fenced compound before the house his wife grew a few four-o'clocks and African marigolds, lovingly cosseted with used water. She was tall, upright, smooth-haired and brown-skinned with that quality of stillness in her repose that comes with Indian blood. One daughter was away at school. Another sat in a beautifully made folding chair, the design of which has not changed since its European original was made in the mid-sixteenth century, trailing delicate fingertips over the armrests with all the aplomb of an infanta. The littlest was feverish. Her hacking cough had been around for too many weeks.

In their vegetable garden, corn, melons, marrows and cucumbers struggled against the looming drought. Already the growing season was almost over. As the cruel sun slid down the sky, and Xuri's trees began to cast long, violet shadows towards the little house, and his wife slipped out with a dish of something for the green parrots that Nordestinos love so well, it seemed a good and dignified life. The cattle and goats clanked past on their way to their stalls. An occasional *vaqueiro* tipped his fringed hat as he rode past. We were the false note, encouraging Xuri to chip away at a *carranca* for the camera. Xuri obeyed silently, but in his eyes I thought I saw the look. His lady patroness, who had led us to him, told us loudly how one *carranqueiro* whom she had rescued from destitution took his first pay-cheque and spent it on drink and drugs, abandoning his hungry family. 'Amazing. These people.' Her house was full of the worst bad art it would ever be possible to see, debased embroideries, abominable carvings, gross daubs of sentimental subjects. Clearly she could see no reason why a man reduced to making a coarse fool of himself in lieu of making an honest living should throw up everything and embrace a slow death. I thought if Xuri did not do such a thing, it was largely because of something I saw in his wife's eyes, a wise, disabused, mischievous twinkle.

As Xuri's patroness could not be prevailed upon to hold her tongue during the filming, she was sent off to take me to visit others of her protégés, a family of lace-makers. Once again I was reluctant, for I had seen the lace, which was a meagre remnant of European tradition, uninteresting and irrelevant to everyday life. The old women, all without men for one reason or another, were supposed to live by their lace-making, but with a metre of lace, a week's work, selling at 300 cruzeiros (about 15p) they clearly did not. Their house was rather grander than Xuri's, for it was faced with brick, and had rooms opening on both sides of the main one, but the beds of the three sisters were all to be found in one room. Another served as a store for their family possessions, and the other two were empty. In the fenced compound

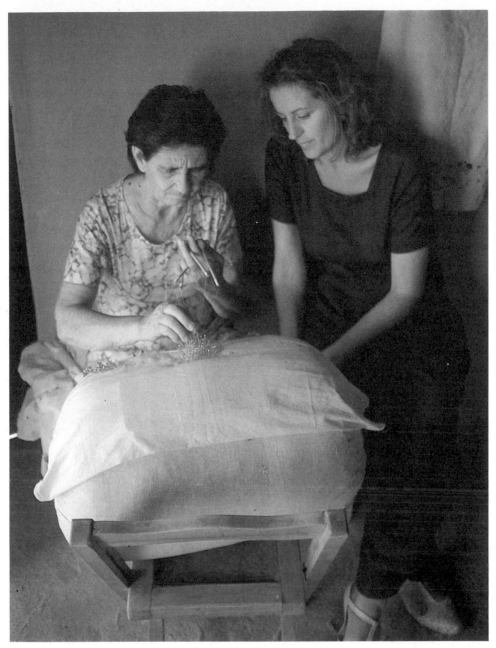
One of the lace-makers shows Germaine Greer her handiwork

behind the house was a low, round mound, about 4 metres across, of smooth quartz pebbles, where washing would be thrown to dry and bleach in the sun, but if the gentle ladies were forced to survive by taking in washing no one mentioned it and I didn't like to ask. It was not until my second visit that I realised how close to going under the old ladies were. Chronic malnutrition is not so easy to detect among the elderly. In their calm and lovely house floored with silver sand brushed every day into a fan pattern, the nunlike sisters with their charming manners were practically starving.

Still trapped in the tourist convention, we went next day to a *vaquejada*, the Brazilian version of a rodeo. A truckload of little steers was penned at the top of a sandy run. At a signal one of them was driven out of the corral and ridden down by two horsemen, one of whom had to grasp the fleeing creature by the tail and flip it on to its back within a zone marked out with flour. Then the fallen steer was pushed or dragged to its feet and driven into another pen, to be reloaded onto the truck and taken back to the corral at the top of the run. By the time we arrived the steers were exhausted. Often they would lie motionless where they were thrown while the riders spurred their horses to trample them into getting to their feet. It seemed impossible that tail-twisting to throw such a heavy animal could be painless. Just as I was making up my mind to stop watching a display which involved little skill and no courage, a fat, bespectacled competitor, a weekend *vaqueiro* if ever there was one, rode up to the judges holding the broken-off end of the steer's tail in his hand. The exposed vertebra shone in the dusty sunlight like a pearl. Another man, involved in some dispute with the judges, did not notice that he had ridden his horse against a dislodged fence-rail so that its legs were on both sides of it and it could not answer the spur. The horse

Vaqueiros chasing a steer at a *vaquejada* near Juàzeiro. Right: the *São Francisco* at Juàzeiro, loaded with wood

tossed its head desperately as the spurs banged into its flanks and the fence-rail gouged its belly. Nobody who relied on his horse for a livelihood could afford to be so stupid. Genuine *vaqueiros* drive their horses hard, and although they use a cruel bit, they are likely to unsaddle and wash their horses from head to foot in precious water before they see to themselves. Everywhere we looked people were showing off, spurring their horses to ride at full pelt into the crowd and pulling them up so short that they reared and almost fell, then turning on a sixpence and dashing off in some other direction, a procedure which seemed to me even more dangerous than it was pointless, especially as the performers were growing steadily drunker. When two of the drunkest began singing improvised songs of praise to the two *prefeites* of Juàzeiro and Petrolina, who sat looking modest and kindly for the camera, it seemed time to go with a vengeance. I longed for the river beyond the dust.

Next morning the *São Francisco* did indeed embark on her last journey up the river she was named for, waddling and shimmying as her gaily painted paddles slapped the water. We were the only passengers, except for a man who said he was a travel agent from Belo Horizonte and two journalists. Life on the river-banks was

very different from life in the *sertão*. Huge mango trees made great pools of shade. Beans, manioc, bananas, papaya and corn shot up out of the ground. Some farmers had diesel pumps. More ran up and down the bank with pails of water; where the bank was steep, steps had been cut in the greyish-pink earth. Small boats were moored at simple landing-stages which women used to bash clothes on. As our majestic bulk hove in sight everyone downed tools and ran to look, laughing, waving, shouting. If I had seen nothing but the river-bank I might have thought that the Valle do Rio São Francisco was a sort of Stephen Foster paradise. As it was I couldn't help marvelling at the luck of the people whose ancestors had settled the narrow alluvial strip. The annual flooding of the river seemed a small price to pay for a life-style which consisted mostly of fishing, with enough tilling of the soil to vary the regime and picking fruit from trees to provide all the vitamins not to be found in beans, manioc and fish. It was mere subsistence, to be sure, but the majority of the people I had observed so far had to struggle desperately hard for a very inferior life. The children who grew up in the riverine *roças* grew strong and tall, but there were

The village of Horto, near Juàzeiro

too many who did not make it, because of enteric disease and parasitic infestation and periodic visitations of *gripe*. The official infant mortality figure is about 160 per thousand live births, but as I roamed around I became aware that lots of little bodies are interred at the corners of fields and no official the wiser. Even that high figure represents considerable under-reporting.

We reached the dam at sunset. Our ramshackle craft was wafted up in a giant lock and we were set free upon the largest man-made lake in the world. It was not meant to be the largest man-made lake in the world, but like Topsy it growed. The dam should have been one of a series of five, but it was simply built a little higher and a little longer and a greater area was flooded. The foreign advisers warned against doing such a thing, but the Brazilians saw that a little daring would pay off in international reputation, so, at the risk of altering the water-levels as far upstream as Bom Jesus da Lapa, they went ahead. The financiers of the project, in particular the International Research and Development Bank, insisted upon resettlement of the riverine population, a notion to which lip-service is as easy as its realisation is difficult. There was no similar land to the rich alluvial strip available. To transplant the river people to the *caatinga* was to condemn them to slow death. Some were moved upstream to settlements called *agrovilas*, the explanation being that south of Bom Jesus da Lapa there was an annual rainfall sufficient for an industrious farmer to survive. In fact the *agrovilas* are strategic hamlets where people from 'foci of social tension' all over Brazil have been resettled, whether the houses have been constructed yet or not. Like the *casas popolares* the *agrovilas* are a perverted project. If they had worked they would have proved a tremendous burden for the state of Bahia to carry. As they have not worked the people have drifted away, to São Paulo and Salvador, to Petrolina and Juàzeiro, to swell the ranks of the landless poor. Many of the marginal cultivators had no official title to their holdings and were neither resettled nor compensated. Others waited so long for their compensation that the inflation rate and their lawyers' fees absorbed it all. A more obvious solution would have been to resettle the people in irrigated land, but irrigated land has to earn its keep in intensive production of cash crops. As CHESF (the São Francisco Hydroelectric Company) points out, it is not a philanthropic organisation. CODEVASF has its irrigation projects, but development means the production of vast quantities of cheap ethanol for the world market; it does not mean the creation of a pampered class of independent farmers with no spending power.

When the waters began to rise, the people who had seen the São Francisco flood many times before could not believe that they would not recede. As they rose and rose, gradually the people realised that the land they called their own had disappeared forever (or until the dam burst, an event some are still praying for).

At midnight the *São Francisco* stopped to take on more wood, so much more wood that the lower deck had room for nothing else. As the last pieces were loaded at first light, we saw thousands of toads, who had retreated as the waters rose, hopping about frantically as their shelter was stripped away. A man and his wife stood watching, as their brood of semi-naked children bashed at the toads with lumps of wood. A few yards up the bank stood a cluster of wretched hovels. CHESF had installed a single electric light on the outside of one of the houses, but it was not on.

133

A member of the crew loads more wood onto the *São Francisco*

For most of the next day we sailed over the dead shallows of the lake. The only events were skeletal tree-tops and the water-tower of old Sento Sé. Scan the shores though I might I could see no sign of life, no house, no animal, no track. Far in the baking distance rose eroded scarps where once there were mines. No roads cut through the grey-green scrub. Later I travelled on the road that CHESF made from Sento Sé to Juàzeiro, and flew over the scrub, marked only by the boundaries of the *fazendeiros'* vast holdings and the scars of cattle traffic round the few water-holes. The day after I drove past the town built by CHESF for the families of the men who worked on the dam, the people who had had nowhere to go when the work was completed, some 2000 of the population of 20,000, sacked the general store, because they were starving. The town had cost a fortune to build; development eighties' style requires its aban- donment rather than an attempt to set up light industry using the cheap power the inhabitants had helped to generate. Everywhere on the Rio São Francisco the same message could be read: people are a luxury. The propaganda put out by CODEVASF, subsidised by Mercedes-Benz do Brasil SA, presented Sobradinho as having two principal functions, flood control and irrigation. A reservoir that is kept full must cause flooding rather than prevent it, and so Sobradinho has done, three times. The river may be more navigable but fewer craft navigate it. The irrigation schemes are available to entrepreneurs who can put up capital for their development, and to them also is available a vast pool of underemployed labour from which to pick and choose the handful who will slave in the fields. For days I sought the flowering promised for the *caatinga* and found only a huge alcohol plant at Casa Nova. I was told there were more fish in the lake and refrigeration plants to keep them in, but I never saw a fishing-boat until we docked at new Sento Sé. As we waddled into the quay we minced its nets with our paddles.

At Sento Sé we were hostages of an extraordinary personage known simply as Father Mark, an American priest from the Middle West, whose ministry seemed to have less to do with spreading the Catholic faith than with inculcating the principles and methodology of private enterprise. He did not insist on hearing confessions before distributing communion in any of his sixty far-flung parishes but gave great attention to bringing his onion crop on at a time when the market supply of onions elsewhere was low and demand high. Consecrated hosts were left in the tabernacles to be handed out by lay helpers, a practice which has become routine in remote parts of Brazil, where the teaching which would help people perhaps to make sense of the chaos and misery in which they live is neglected.

Father Mark had secured a prime piece of irrigable land in replacement for the diocesan lands now submerged, and he put a great deal of his own and other people's energy into making it work. His American supporters sent him $15,000 or $20,000 a year which he carefully husbanded without too punctilious a concern for the Brazilian currency regulations. His work-force was not composed of the workless adults of new Sento Sé but of school-age boys and girls, the titular owners of the land, who lived in dormitories in the presbytery compound. The accommodation was spartan. Boys slept four or five to a small, bare room, folding up their hammocks by day and storing their belongings in trunks or boxes. The toilet facilities were primitive and over the whole hung the nauseating smell of fermenting manioc. In the manioc factory there was no attempt at dust control and no safety guards on any of the machines. The irrigation channels on the farm were unlined: evidently Father Mark believes that God will hold salinisation at bay in the interests of the private-enterprise system.

It was clear, looking at his land which was the best for miles, that the *sertão* needs more than water to make it bloom. There was no humus whatsoever in the neutral soil in which the precious water sank away at once. On the other side of the lake, people tainted with socialist beliefs (the gospel of hate, according to Father Mark) seemed to be doing rather better in the development stakes, for the town of Remanso was ringed with irrigated fields.

By now we were becoming aware that there was nothing normal in the apparition of a *gaiola* at the ports on the Rio São Francisco. When we stopped at Xique Xique, a town totally surrounded by an enormous wall built by CHESF, further evidence that the level of the river was permanently raised beyond the boundaries of the lake, ordinary life came to a dead halt. We walked through streets virtually deserted because most adults and all the children were standing spellbound on the wall. No sooner did the crew put down the gangplank than people swarmed on board, all screaming with delight and amazement, jamming the companionways. They continued pouring on and off until the *São Francisco* blew her steam-whistle threateningly; then the scream leapt the octave and they threw themselves on land, terrified that they would be borne off into the unknown. At Barra, a delightful town built by the cattle barons to a standard to which CHESF had never aspired, with piped water and paved streets and a meat market as clean as an operating theatre, and at Ibotirama, a sprawling, filthy brothel town growing up at the point where the Salvador–Brasília highway crosses the river, the scene was repeated, on an ever-expanding scale, until our journey southwards took on the aspect of a Götterdämmerung. Pieces cracked or shattered or fell off the engine. The brightly painted funnel turned black and at one point burst into flames. Leaks opened in all systems. Hot water failed and lavatories refused to flush. Worst of all, the wood kept running out, as it took more and more to generate a head of steam. We were falling so far behind schedule there was only one thing to do. The BBC temporarily abandoned the ageing prima donna and travelled overland to Bom Jesus da Lapa, thereby running a considerable risk of not being on hand when the old girl finally sank or burned to the water-line.

Bom Jesus is a centre of religious tourism, simply because there is a series of large caverns to be found under a rock outcrop so tall that it can be seen from miles downriver. Any landmark in Brazil is instantly claimed for the Church and sur-mounted with a statue or a cross. Bom Jesus not only crowned the heights, but created a Via Crucis up through the rock sugar-loaf and filled the underground caverns with altars and shrines. The whole complex has now been taken over by a group of Polish priests whose interpretation of the economic application of God's law is markedly different from Father Mark's, for they are earnestly working for the Commissão Pastoral da Terra, which is struggling to organise and mobilise rural workers to defend their rights. A few weeks before we arrived an independent farmer who had been resisting continual harassment for years, refusing to abandon his *roça*, had been shot by a group of gunmen, in front of witnesses. The police had been strangely unable to connect the assassins with his persecutor, the *fazendeiro*. The women who survived him had no stomach for continuing the struggle. When I saw one of the priests talking with a group of peasants after mass, I followed them to the church hall. It was the first of May, the *dia do trabalhador*, but in the hall were only old men and schoolgirls, who listened hypnotised to the earnest harangues of the young politicos, one of whom had flown from Salvador specially for the meeting. The discourse was impassioned, the language that of infant Marxism with frequent

Above: a Nordestino house made of wattle and daub. Right: a market scene in Juàzeiro

Above: a family of basket-weavers. Previous page: Germaine Greer on board the stern-wheeler *São Francisco*

A lace-maker working at home in Juàzeiro

Above: the final touch: fitting the *carranca* to the *São Francisco*
Left: children are much loved in Brazil. The baby was unofficially adopted by this already poor family

The River São Francisco flows past fields of manioc

Above: a group of young workers waiting for the boat onto which they will load the pumpkins they have collected from the fields. Right: Penedo, near the mouth of the River São Francisco

A stoker feeding the fire-box on the *São Francisco*

The stern paddle-wheel on the *São Francisco*

references to *a luta da classe*, but the Polish priest, who listened and carefully refrained from taking over the meeting, even when the leaders got into a tangle about minutes and motions, did not flinch. The *trabalhadores rurais* close to Bom Jesus are either *vaqueiros* or dependants of the beef industry and the good graces of the *fazendeiros*, who had neither been to mass nor the meeting. Communications are so bad in the interior of Bahia that there was no way farmers in the back blocks could get to Bom Jesus. The little meeting with its fine rhetoric and its high ideals represented no threat to the *status quo* whatever. We were committed to film an annual festival in Bom Jesus, which we had already been asked to subsidise. We managed to talk our way out of it, almost, although the festival went ahead with dreadful inevitability, but the little meeting was in its way as unreal to me as the *fiesta*. I felt as if the Nordeste was fading away before my eyes. The only real thing was the great yellow river, writhing in its bonds.

The religion of Bahia is a mixture of *candomblé*, a form of voodoo, and Catholicism. Here Germaine Greer examines articles and medicines at a *candomblé* stall at Bom Jesus da Lapa

We travelled up to Pirapora where brown boys caught the fish that flipped like coins out of the rapids, and no tourists bought *carrancas* or danced at the discothèque. I rejoined the old *gaiola* after spending seven hours slipping downstream in a tiny boat and slept one more night in my cabin which boomed and banged as the crew flung the last of the forests of wood she had consumed into her voracious boiler. At noon next day she nosed into the smelly mud-flat by the São Francisco Navigation Company's workshops in Pirapora and the boilers were shut down. All along the bank people had downed tools and run to follow her, effortlessly keeping up with her crippled pace. Reporters appeared from nowhere, one with a cine camera, for all the world as though she had been a real ship on a real voyage. The sailors changed into dazzling whites. There was no sign in their confident greetings that from now on they were out of work. They held up their children to be kissed and admired, lavishing on them all the caresses that they did not give to their wives. Other Latins might leave everything to *mañana*; the Nordestino adores and indulges his children because he knows that the only good time of their lives is today. How can there be a future with inflation running at 120 per cent a year? Why teach children self-denial when there is no jam tomorrow? Why lower an astronomical birth-rate when it will take twice as many children to keep you in your old age as it has taken your parents? Why teach the work ethic when there is no work? Better far to frolic in the river catching a hundred minnows than to learn useless skills in an expensive school or nothing at all in a free one.

Pirapora is in the state of Minas Gerais which is industrialised in the Brazilian manner, which is to say that its metal production depends upon charcoal for smelting. Hundreds and hundreds of hectares grow nothing but trash eucalypts, planted so closely that from a distance they look like dull-green Axminster. There is no space to walk between or beneath them. For this cultivation, too, people are irrelevant. From Minas Gerais we went to the fertile coastal plain at the mouth of the river, to Penedo with its gaily painted Portuguese colonial houses, and its sick children. When I asked why children died so often, the people laughed the genuine laugh mirthless. Of the three men who crewed the *canoa* which took me upstream to Pão de Azucar, one was unmarried, one had had seven children of whom three were alive, and the other had had five, all dead. It is not an easy matter to talk to people of their lost children. Generally the older people were convinced that matters had improved greatly. Certainly, the polio immunisation campaign had been efficiently run, and malaria, even if it is resurgent, is not the scourge it once was, but the people's optimism was fragile, more like an aspect of good manners than a spontaneous feeling. Medical services existed only in theory; public free clinics were either closed or manned by incompetents, or so they thought. The people's teeth were terrible, but a filling cost 15,000 or 20,000 cruzeiros. Nobody wore glasses, including two of our drivers who could not discern turnings until they were right on top of them, but they struggled on somehow. The people's mad optimism began to get to me so that I wanted to shake them and say, 'For God's sake get angry!' but I knew that anger would only make them less able to endure.

Perhaps the worst moment was when a young couple came into a clinic with their two children, a new-born who was frantic with hunger but by now so weak that his cry was beginning to fail, and a little girl who could not walk for weakness and a pain in her buttock, but lay with her head on her father's shoulder, gazing sightlessly with eyes glazed with fever. The doctor (whose only qualification was in dentistry) did not notice the new-born's futile sucking movements and did not ask the mother about her milk until prompted. She laughed and said she had very little, and laughed again when she said she was giving the child cow's milk. 'Make sure you dilute it with water,' said the doctor. The village had no water-treatment plant; she might as well have diluted the milk with cyanide. The doctor did not tell her to boil either the milk or the water. The little girl seemed to me to have polio, but the doctor did not ask if they had had her vaccinated. He treated her for worms instead. Her father kept crazily trying to cheer her up, bouncing her and joking with her, calling her 'mulher' and flirting. The mother pounded her new-born on the back and laughed again as she told the doctor that she had already had a child die. She herself was only twenty.

I left Penedo and drove overland through the fertile coastal plain, most of it given over to sugar cultivation for ethanol production, and into the area of intensive mixed cultivation called *agreste*. Here the population was dense, and large, sprawling towns with advanced light industry appeared at every crossroads, but just as suddenly they gave way to the *sertão*, and I was back in the São Francisco heartland. Here in the state of Alagoas, cattle-raising was more intensive than in Bahia. Every inch of the dry, inhospitable hills was used. Tiny houses were everywhere. I saw water-trucks drawn by oxen and women washing in every mantled pool or runlet of green water. As we swooped over a rise, I saw coming out of one of the low mud houses a flock of women in clean, bright dresses, red, pink and turquoise. I turned in my seat, thinking I was seeing something like a Nordestino Tupperware party. 'A funeral,' said the driver. Then I saw among the skirts that flickered in the breeze two little girls carrying a cardboard box with improvised handles. 'Why are they all women?' I asked, being more familiar with countries where only men attend funerals. 'The deceased was a woman,' said the driver, letting in the clutch. A woman 18 inches long. I have seen infant death in many places, but never has it seemed more appalling than that brisk little procession, making its way to the walled cemetery where bare mound was heaped on bare mound, with no time for grass to grow, or to make a cross or to name the mounds.

I went on to Paulo Afonso, where a series of huge hydroelectric stations harvest the power from the river yoked at Sobradinho. I was guided up and down inside the vast fabric, into the shadowless bowels where a handful of men presided over the electrification of all the cities of the Nordeste. I was shown the oasis where the élite CHESF workers are housed among fountains and exotic trees. I was shown the zoo where Brazil's original inhabitants die slowly in their own stink. It seemed a world away from that line of women making their way over the bare hill. The technical achievement of Paulo Afonso is staggering; piping water to the struggling farmers of Alagoas is a doddle by comparison. I went to Brasília to find out what plans if any the central government has for this region. The senior official who spoke with me was charming. Yes, the Nordeste was discriminated against and probably on racist grounds. Yes, the Nordeste had chiefly functioned as a reservoir of cheap labour for the developed south. On the other hand I must understand that even in the fertile plain near the river-mouth the initial cost of the rice polders was $12,000 per hectare. There was no way such an investment could be put in the hands of backward farmers with no knowledge of or aptitude for intensive, year-round cultivation. If irrigation was developed, it would have to be done by the states in collaboration with private investors. No, such schemes would not make very much difference to the unemployment picture. As for bringing river-water to the *poligono das secas*, academics had made many plans, but state and local politics are involved, and like federal politics, he smiled, these are dominated by vested interests. In Brazil the same people own the land, the money and the power. But it was true that the river was a priceless national resource and should not be allowed to become nothing but a conduit of kinetic energy, hence the existence of PLANVASF which would co-ordinate SUDENE, CODEVASF, PORTOBRAS, CHESF, CEMIG and DNAEE and the Ministries of Agriculture and Mines and Energy . . . a new acronym to add to the storm of acronyms which designates Brazil's bureaucracy. 'The most likely result of attempting to co-ordinate all the authorities dealing with the river in any of its aspects is a number of very long and inconclusive meetings,' I said. 'Precisely,' said my friend from the Ministry of the Interior, and again he smiled. He was a very nice man, but he knew and I knew that the people of the Rio São Francisco had had it. They could continue to struggle in a declining, outmoded, second-rate beef industry, or they could cling to their scraps of earth, or they could take the journey to the *favelas* of the overcrowded cities which so many of their kin had taken before them, never to return.

People crammed into *favelas* lose their trustfulness and the spontaneity of their smiles, and all the other qualities that make the Nordestino people so special. I said goodbye to the river at Bom Jesus da Lapa, where the setting sun turned the water to copper. Small boys twirled their throwing nets which, as they dropped, broke up the red shimmer in flakes of verdigris. Soft brown women leaned on the parapet talking and laughing round their babies' prying fingers, squeezing their brown bottoms in their hands. The people rich enough to have proper houses with electricity were sitting spellbound by the soap operas, while their children played among the pig and dog droppings in the street. Watching the technicolor posturing of a fictitious middle class surrounded by the impedimenta of conspicuous consumption through tumbledown doorways in a street full of scummy water and decomposing excrement, I was shocked to find myself hoping that Padre Damiano was right; perhaps the dam would burst, and the bloated river become its wild self again. The people had learned to live with the river's changes. Now that the river was controlled by man's caprice and greed, there was no coming to terms with it.

THE MURRAY
Russell Braddon

My river journey began in the late spring on top of one of Australia's higher mountains. By world standards a rather low mountain, it was high enough to be wearing a shawl of unseasonable snow. Frozen, I stood ankle-deep in the shawl's fraying hem and watched a trickle of water from its icy fringe wander down the mountain's shoulder. The Murray's enigmatic, 1700-mile trek to the sea had begun.

I won't pretend that my first glimpse of that feeble trickle affected me profoundly. What I actually thought was that, unless it quickly became navigable, I had a long walk ahead of me; that I was singularly ill-shod to walk through snow about which no one had had the courtesy to warn me; and that, despite the cold, I was thirsty. A hundred yards farther on, the infant Murray offered me a drink from what had already become a rill of the sweetest water imaginable.

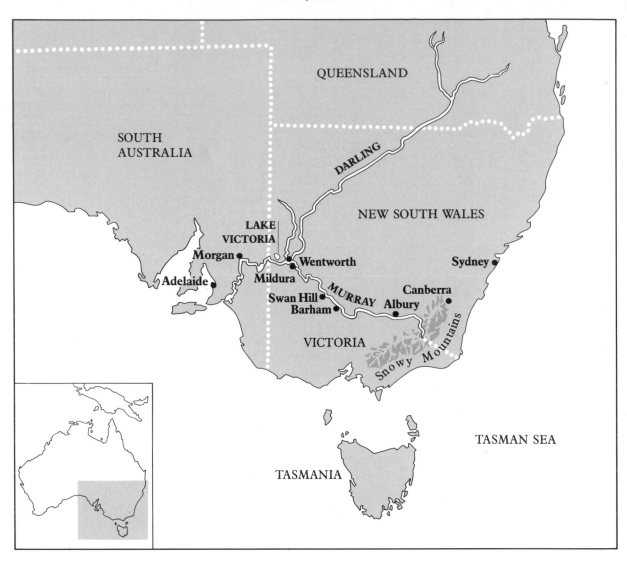

Walking on toward the tree-line, the ground was springy and thickly carpeted with coarse, avocado-coloured grass. When I lay on it, it felt like a warm, spongy mattress. And as I lay, a horseman breasted the mountain's shoulders at a fast canter. He wore a bush hat and a long, yellowish waterproof cape. Nolan should have painted him – and 'Banjo' Paterson certainly had his like in mind when he wrote of Australia's legendary horseman, in his ballad *The Man from Snowy River*.

For some reason, we Australians *need* legendary figures in our recent past, need to see their tough, outdoor likeness in our indoor, urban selves. Which may be the reason why I – a metropolitan creature who craves the company of anonymous millions, and loathes the country – decided to make this journey. That and the fact that, since she entered the so-called European Community, Britain has disowned me, Australia regards me as a scab for continuing to work there, and I am beginning to feel dispossessed. Perhaps, I thought, the Murray would teach me as much about

150

myself and my roots as it would about her geography. About her geography, though, she would have to teach me everything. I am not of that school that reads all the literature before travelling to unknown places, and had come to the Murray with a mind not so much ill-informed as blank. Very sensibly, too, because almost immediately the cantering horseman reined his sure-footed nag to a halt and joined me for a chat – or, as he put it, a yarn. He told me that it was these very mountains that had delayed the expansion of the cramped convict colony on the coast of New South Wales for forty years. They had loomed unnaturally blue to the near west of the colony beyond a forest of gaunt gums between whose grey trunks flitted the figures of naked and doubtless savage blacks. To European eyes, whose one tenuous link with home was the ocean, Australia's coastal belt was mysterious enough: what lay beyond its mountains, and spread for 3000 miles until it reached another ocean, seemed too daunting even to contemplate. It is one of history's most curious ironies that the world's oldest inhabitable landmass, its largest and potentially richest island, was the last to be discovered and has been one of the slowest to be developed.

But after Napoleon's defeat at Waterloo, there being nowhere Britons dared not then go, nothing that they couldn't then do, the era of the Great British Walkabout was born. Through every uncharted jungle, desert and heathen land Britons thereupon beat their blithe tracks and greeted one another, when their tracks crossed, with such marvels of understatement as, 'Dr Livingstone, I presume.'

As if by osmosis, their mood reached the penal settlement of Sydney. The daunting mountains were promptly crossed, and the Murray was discovered – twice. Close to its source, the first time, and hundreds of miles downstream, where it is joined by the Murrumbidgee, the second time, by Sturt, who later followed her course all the way to the sea.

Further hundreds of miles downstream, it turned out also to be joined by what was later named the Darling – whose source lay 1000 miles to the north. Together, the three rivers wound their respective ways through 3000 miles of plainland. Once discovered, they quickly became the principal means of expansion in a country that had no railways and very few roads.

And so the Murray joined what Britain deemed her family of great rivers – the Nile, the Ganges, the Yangtze, the St Lawrence, and so on. Compared with her sisters, however, she was an unglamorous creature, a working-class girl about whom Victorian England preferred to hear nothing; whom Australians, as was their wont with women, were quick to exploit, but respected only when she got nasty.

In the first years of Queen Victoria's reign, they came to her banks and staked their claims. They came on horseback, by bullock wagon and on foot. They forded the river, swam it, or were ferried across it. They came alone or with wives and children. They brought with them seed to sow, a few cattle, an axe and a rifle. And when they found their claim to the land pre-empted by armies of gum-trees and patrols of roving aborigines, they chopped down the trees and evicted or shot the blacks.

Meantime, indifferent to the antics of mere people, the Murray annually flooded black and white alike, purging her sluggish innards of the previous year's snags and silt. And up her shallow waters, quite soon, came paddle-wheeled steamers, skippered, as often as not, by ocean-going European sailors who had jumped ship at Port Augusta in South Australia. Broad of beam and shallow of draught, these paddle-wheelers bore provisions upstream from Adelaide for sale to inland settlers, took back wool and grain for shipment to England, brought pioneering immigrants from Britain and Ireland, missionaries to convert the aboriginals and rebuke the drunken settlers, even Chinese coolies to work the new-found gold-fields.

Thus, in the space of only a few decades, a third of a million square miles of farm-land was added to the habitable territories of Queensland, New South Wales, Victoria and South Australia, and the mood of the Murray became a sure barometer of the prosperity of each. If she flooded excessively, or dried up vindictively – and she did both with great regularity – economic disasters followed. When she was benign, flocks prospered, harvests flourished, paddle-steamers by the hundred threshed 1000 miles upstream and 1000 miles back, and cattlemen drove their herds up onto the mountain-tops every summer, there to graze.

The farmers claimed this annual migration rested their properties along the river-flats, and refreshed their cattle. It also bred 'Banjo' Paterson's legendary horsemen, who mustered their cattle through densely wooded gorges and up rocky passes to the heights, taught each herd its territory, built makeshift huts, lived on meat, damper (bushman's bread) and tea, and spent their evenings around a camp-fire, drinking rum and sweetened condensed milk, and yarning outrageously. But in 1968 the New South Wales Government banned the annual muster. Now, where once the Snowy River horsemen reigned, ski instructors and Rangers rule, tending tourists, sightseers and traffic-stricken wombats rather than cattle. At its very source, the Murray had given me my first intimation that *white* Australia's pioneering spirit was moribund, if not dead.

The mountain-top's trickle had meantime become a stream, bounding puppy-like downhill through drizzling rain and swirling mist. I plodded damply behind it, glumly contemplating the night to come in a one-man tent. I camped on a grassy bank beside what is normally a smiling creek. It had become a sullen torrent. Long years of devastating drought having recently ended, the Murray, on which I was supposed to start a tranquil journey by canoe, was in riotous flood. No one had told me that my great river journey would begin freezingly and continue perilously. So I cheated, put my canoe on top of a van, and drove beside the narrow, snarling torrent until it had broadened into a river barging its rude way between New South Wales and Victoria at a mere 11 miles an hour.

Taking to my canoe only then, I discovered that any idiot could do it. Further-more, canoeing was both restful and serene. Willows brought from England and planted a century ago trailed green fingers in the brown water; white cockatoos stared down at me with unblinking contempt from the grey branches of overhanging gums; black swans swam majestically ahead of me in monogamous pairs; and the Murray herself – all whorls, eddies and mysterious bubbles – rolled fatly between lush banks she was for the moment too indolent to overflow.

As well as being fat and swollen, there was something mysterious about her (I had by now decided that she was neither an it nor a he) that defied my powers of description. *Roget's Thesaurus* might have provided the appropriate synonym, but I'd not brought mine with me, and I doubted I'd find one in Jingellic, which was my next port of call. So, while I waited for the right word, I paddled quietly along at a pace that was mine, but with a rhythm dictated entirely by the Murray.

It was surprising to realise that as well as that indefinable mood, the Murray *had* a rhythm. But no Strauss to capture it, as the Danube had had. Nor a Wagner to dramatise it, as had the Rhine. Nor ancient temples and historic monuments to popularise it, as do the Nile, the Thames and the Seine. Poor Murray! No wonder she held me at arm's length – the more so since I had never even pretended to like her.

Then and there I made a sincere effort at least to admire her. But all I saw was a swirling, muddy stream. It was golden carp that had made it muddy, a farmer told me. Introduced in the sixties by an Italian immigrant and since become a pest, he said, same as rabbits, which were introduced by a pommy. And prickly pear and dozens of plants the cattle were supposed to like, but in fact hated, like Paterson's curse and bugger prickles.

'Watch out downstream for bugger prickles,' he warned. 'Look like thistledown but sting like red-hot needles. And keep your eye out for snakes. This time of the year, the river's swarming with them.' I watched him drive away in his Landrover, across his lush green paddocks, past his herd of fat black cattle, a late-twentieth-century farmer. But I identified with him no more than I did with the bushranger, Mad Dog Morgan, who was said to have preyed on that area in earlier times, holding up isolated pubs and forcing their female staff to dance naked on table-tops. Instead of admiring the Murray, I found myself wondering why Morgan and his odious ilk – of whom Ned Kelly was the epitome – are admired rather than detested by my compatriots. It could be because we're so appallingly overgoverned, I supposed – by one Federal and no less than seven state administrations. Despising politicians and loathing policemen as we do, it is perhaps not entirely perverse of us to admire bushrangers.

One of the Murray's functions, of course, is to separate New South Wales from Victoria. As one paddles downstream, New South Wales is on one's right, Victoria on one's left; but whether the actual border is the left bank or the right, or some invisible line between the two, no one has ever been able to decide. Meantime, because it was the first colony to be established, New South Wales has called itself The Premier State, Victoria has retaliated by dubbing itself The Garden State (as if New South Wales were full of weeds), and South Australia has assumed the title of The Festival State (as if both New South Wales and Victoria were joyless and uncultured). Like three shrewish sisters, Australia's south-eastern states shrilly proclaim their allegedly unique virtues; and like many another hard-working mother, the Murray gets on with the job of feeding her ungrateful brood, and ignores their vain and unseemly squabbles. She has known their habitat for millions of years; they have known it for less than two centuries.

She has been unable, however, to avoid the consequences of those squabbles that concerned the means whereby her greedy daughters sought to exploit her generosity. Because she was vital to the well-being of each – sustaining a vast food basin in two of them and providing the third's supply of fresh water – New South Wales, Victoria and South Australia long ago agreed to create a system of locks and dams which would ensure that her priceless waters did not flow wastefully into the sea, but would be so conserved, even in times of intense drought, as to make constant irrigation *and* navigation possible.

South Australia fulfilled her part of the bargain: New South Wales and Victoria fulfilled only those parts of it which were to their advantage. In other words, they built the dams which have since provided them with a reliable system of irrigation, but reneged on the construction of most of the promised locks – and thereby rendered much of *their* two-thirds of the Murray unnavigable, and the Darling inaccessible. Which is why I was paddling a canoe, instead of lounging in comfort on a paddle-steamer. Yet I was enjoying myself. The last time I had seen the river – during the drought – it had been little more than a drain between whose deep, dry, eroded banks a trickle of water ran from one stagnant pool to the next. On both banks, the willows had been leafless and apparently dead; and to either side the farmlands had been bare, and the cattle that roamed them mere skin and bone. But now the river lapped both banks and had even overflowed them in places to create hundreds of green billabongs; the willows drooped under their burden of emerald leaves; the country-side was carpeted with grass so green it looked unreal; the cattle were glossy and plump; and areas that had been impossible to *give* away even two months ago had again become so prosperous that only millionaires could buy them.

The overflow from the Murray River creates a small billabong

In the past, whenever I had wanted to rediscover Australia, I had gone to a beach and looked out at the ocean. Now, on the Murray, I perceived that Australia belonged less to the sea than to her inland rivers. Moved by this thought, I glanced around at the countryside – whose loneliness had always alienated me – with an almost affectionate eye. And observed that the late-afternoon sun was on my left. Had been on my left for days. I was heading *north*. Yet the water was flowing *down*hill. I marvelled at the cleverness of nature. And, despite the explanations of contemptuous friends, have continued to marvel. Whatever they say, south is down and north is up; and, by defying this fundamental law of gravity, the Murray proves herself not only benevolent but miraculous as well.

Encountering a fisherman on the bank, I asked him if he had caught anything. 'Only bloody carp,' he told me. Apparently the by now ubiquitous (and inedible) carp have destroyed the ecology of the river, turning the hitherto clear waters an opaque brown by stirring up the mud on its floor. All of which has decimated the Murray's once thriving schools of huge and very edible freshwater cod. 'Only way to catch cod now is with *square* hooks,' he said, and looked so sour I didn't dare ask how a square hook could catch anything. I paddled away, leaving him murdering yet another of the handsome, hated, golden carp – because it is illegal to throw them back into the river.

As leisurely as I, but infinitely more purposefully, the Murray writhed her way through the flatlands, heading inexorably uphill until she could at last turn inland and westwards – which would at least be flat! Apparently disgruntled by the effort, her brown, good-natured face had become leaden and sullen. Suddenly, she reminded me of that river down which Humphrey Bogart and Katharine Hepburn were navigating the *African Queen* just before they were hurled into the abyss of a rapid.

Lacking Miss Hepburn's high-chinned courage, I had no desire to be hurled into an abyss. And noticing an isolated building on the right bank – the first for miles, so it had to be a pub – I gave my paddle a confident flick to starboard. Nothing happened. Except that my canoe gathered speed and began to career no less inexorably than the Murray toward invisible but imminent rapids. Willows flashed by me, sneering, and a kookaburra cackled with unseemly mirth. I paddled dementedly. But continued to career downstream, straight as an arrow, toward disaster. Then, almost casually, my canoe swung rightward under the branch of an indifferent gum and hit the grassy bank. Furious (with myself as much as with the river), I grabbed my shirt, haversack and sneakers and disembarked. Needing a spare hand to drag the canoe up the bank, I clenched one of my sneakers between my teeth. Then, haversack in one hand, shirt and one sneaker in the other, the second sneaker between my teeth, I marched into the pub.

It was not a sight to which the locals were accustomed. All conversation ceased. Every eye turned unblinkingly toward me. I didn't care. I had escaped death by a hair's breadth. Before I proceeded another inch down that treacherous river I wanted a drink, and information. Thrusting my way to the bar, I dropped my haversack, took the sneaker from between my teeth, placed it on the counter, and ordered a Coca-Cola. The local who sat to windward of my sneaker winced. Apologising, I dumped it on the floor, put on my shirt and asked about the river.

'Very dangerous,' I was told. 'Rocks.'

I had no greater a desire to be smashed to a pulp on rocks than I had to plunge to my death over rapids. My canoe was light; perhaps I could port it. Through the bugger prickles and snakes.

'Snakes?' I asked.

'Millions of 'em.'

Silence fell again. And the stares remained unblinking. 'What's this I hear about square hooks?' I asked. Instantly, their po faces broke into cunning smiles and the silence became a babble of banter. 'Square hooks are a no-no,' they told me. 'You don't talk about square hooks here.'

Square hooks, it turned out, were nets. And illegal. But widely used in pursuit of the now elusive cod. Of which, amid much conviviality, I had a large portion for lunch. The licensee – an emigrant from Sydney, from whose drugs and violence she had brought her young family to the safe fresh air of the country – cooked it for me; and I had the good manners *not* to ask how she had obtained it.

I left Jingellic's isolated pub to a chorus of good-natured farewells, and loaded my canoe onto another van. For the next hour I surveyed the Murray from the front seat of a vehicle in which there were no snakes and on a road devoid of unseen perils. But rattling along at 120 kilometres an hour, shouting small talk above the din of a cassette blaring rock music, I found myself missing the serenity of the river.

So I rejoined it where its pace had slackened almost to a standstill, its width increased to a mile, its depth to 40 feet and its surface become a sheet of bronze cellophane. I was paddling westwards at last, to the distant weir of the Hume Dam.

It was dawn, a light mist rose from the water, the light was soft, the surrounding hillsides glowed purple with their mantle of Paterson's curse, the water was like glass, only drips from my paddle broke the silence, and it *should* have been beautiful. Instead, it was eerie. Partly because this was a man-made lake, but mostly because, when he had made it, man had dammed the valley but not removed its trees. Now – bleached and lifeless – their trunks reared above the water that had drowned them. The billions of gallons of water retained behind the high wall of the Hume Weir looked less like a dam than the no-man's-land of an aquatic Passchendaele.

Even so, it had improved beyond belief on what it had been when years of drought had almost emptied it. Then, it had looked like Nagasaki after its devastation by an atomic bomb. Yet it had served its purpose. Symbol of man's inhumanity to Nature it may be, but for five almost rainless years its reserves of water had kept the vast food basin of orchards and vineyards below it irrigated and alive.

Standing atop the dam's high wall – water at my heels, a dizzy drop before me – I gazed down at an unrecognisable Murray. Below and beyond the weir's massive wall it had become not so much a river as a maze of creeks and billabongs. A man in a canoe could vanish in that lot. Crocodiles notwithstanding, I'd rather have paddled through Florida's swamps.

So what to do? How to see *all* of this river, when this sector of it was miles from any road and a death-trap to boot? It was at dinner that night, in a Mexican restaurant, that the answer came to me. If I couldn't drive beside it, and wouldn't paddle through it, I could at least fly over it.

The following morning found me at the local airport. In a trice I was taking off in a

Cessna; and in a further trice we were banking over the maze of creeks, billabongs and islands. 'You could get yourself lost down there,' commented the pilot who, despite his Australian accent, was Italian. The Murray, it occurred to me, still attracted the adventurous. But rarely from those who lived beside it. A Sydney publican, a Mexican restaurateur, an Italian pilot. Maybe it was coincidence. Time and the rest of my journey would tell.

The maze ended and from it a single river emerged, broad, brown and incredibly serpentine. Viewing it from the air had been a good idea, but the roar of the Cessna's engine was somehow incongruous. A glider would have been better.

I hired one at Tocumwal. It had been manufactured in Bulgaria, my pilot came from Sweden, and viewing the Murray from the air in silence was an improvement. Nor could I any longer doubt that the Murray was a mighty river. Not only was she thrusting her dauntless way westward, she and the early pioneers who had travelled up, or trekked to, her had transformed the plains on either side of her into rich farmland.

The sandy-beached bends – once the bugbear of the paddle-boat skippers towing barges laden with wool or wheat – were now the haunt of summer tourists; and Echuca, in the distance, once Australia's greatest inland port, was now a lovingly restored monument to our so-called national heritage. In its heyday, Echuca's lofty, tiered wharf could accommodate six paddle-steamers and their attendant barges. Since no less than 200 steamers were plying the river, there was always a queue of other boats waiting their turn to be unloaded of their cargo of stores and reladen with bales of wool and wheat.

The banks of the Murray River at Echuca

The paddle-steamer *Pevensey* moored by the wharves at Echuca

Today, Echuca's handful of steamers ply only a few miles up and down the river, and carry sightseers. But a local Historical Society has accepted the thankless task of restoring both the wharf and the hulks of vessels abandoned when the railways put them out of business and of putting on record the colourful adventures of steamers long since vanished and skippers long since dead. These tales are legion, and their impact is in no way diminished by the fact that each has several versions. Whatever the version, they all concern nineteenth-century enterprise and the unpredictability of the Murray. Thus, the skipper who was delivering a tombstone for the grave of a recently deceased wife: en route, the river fell, the steamer was grounded and it was two years before the river rose again. By the time the tombstone was delivered another had been installed and the widower had remarried. In its alternative version, the steamer was carrying timber for the construction of a church. By the time it arrived, the church was completed. So the skipper took his unwanted cargo hundreds of miles upstream to Bourke, where it was used to build a pub.

Nothing ventured, nothing gained was always the motto of the river-boat skipper, but enterprise was not always rewarded. By shipping railway sleepers upstream, for example, he eventually ruined himself. And the penalty for excessive daring was always that his vessel was grounded by the receding flood.

During a major flood, the Murray could be as wide in places as 200 miles – or so vows one of its few surviving old-timers. Two hundred miles or a mere 50, a vast area of farmland was inundated. And threading their way between tall red gums, whose wood they used to feed their voracious boilers, the shallow-draught steamers and barges would rescue flocks of sheep and herds of cattle. But if, during this operation, the waters went down, the animals were simply disembarked, to resume their grazing, and the steamer and its barges were left high and dry to rot.

The mini-paddle-steamer, *Emmy Lou*

Meantime, the paddle-steamers bore *human* cargoes upstream: men and women no less adventurous than the buccaneering skippers, but bent on making their fortune on dry land. All would slave, many would be destroyed by the next and inevitable drought, but every one of them had been lured inland by the promising but uncompromising Murray.

To whose brown bosom it was high time I returned; but this time in luxury. I boarded the mini-paddle-steamer, *Emmy Lou*, which was built – to his own specification, with his own hands, and those of a group of loyal supporters – by a mild-looking, bespectacled Englishman called Anthony Bowell. Bored by his successful career in publicity in London, Anthony had sought a new challenge in Australia. No less bored by his success as a publicity man and photographer in Sydney, he had decided to travel the full length of the Darling by raft. That feat achieved, he had decided to build a small paddle-steamer capable of accommodating fourteen passengers, and then to challenge the Murray.

He knew no more about boat-building, steam-engines, navigation or the Murray than the average photographer and publicity man, but, quite undeterred, he found an old steam-engine in a sawmill; lugged it 60 miles to Barham, on the banks of the Murray; dismantled, modified and restored it; laid a keel; constructed a steel hull; added decking, a wheel-house, cabins and paddle-wheels; hired a skipper and engineer, a purser and a chef; put them all (except the chef, who wore traditional garb) in open-necked white shirts and black trousers; and took to the river.

All he needed then, because his savings had gone and his home was heavily mort-gaged, was passengers. Deservedly, there have been plenty of them. When I met him, however, he was looking for a new challenge.

I offered him one – to take me from Echuca to Swan Hill, which was probably impossible, because I knew much of that long stretch was navigable only when the Murray was in flood, and when it was in flood, the telephone cables and the bridge across the river at Barham would foul both the *Emmy Lou*'s wheel-house and her funnel.

'I'll get you there,' Anthony promised. 'Even if we have to dismantle the wheel-house and saw a foot or so off the funnel.'

The two-day journey to Barham was restful, but never dull. At its outset we passed the *Pevensey*, a paddle-wheeled work-horse of the early days, heading up-stream. Its skipper, who looked as if he had been on the river all his life, was a Sydney-born man who had served in the RAAF during the war, become a chemist afterwards, and bought a pharmacy in Echuca. His crew, who looked thoroughly disreputable, were respected local businessmen. But the *Pevensey*, like Echuca's wharf, no longer worked for her living; she was one of the town's many restored monuments to the recent past.

Leaving her astern, we rounded a bend. Then another, another and another, every bend the same, every stretch ahead of each bend exactly like the last. Thousands upon thousands of red gums up to their grateful knees in mile upon mile of restless water. Hundreds upon hundreds of pumps, idle now, but ready to fill their attendant irrigation channels the instant the flood receded. Herds of cows, irritated by our

The *Pevensey* chugs down the Murray River

The Murray River near Corryong with the Snowy Mountains in the distance

Hume Weir near Albury

Summer tourists enjoy a backwater of the Murray River near Corowa

The small paddle-steamer *Emmy Lou*

The Murray River swamps bush land near Mildura

The *Murray Explorer* berthed between Mildura and Morgan

The confluence of the Murray River and the River Darling at Wentworth

approach, lumbered shoulder to shoulder towards us, as if to repel invasion. Pigs bounded inquisitively to the water's edge, like escapees from Orwell's *Animal Farm* determined to ask impertinent questions. Pin-headed kangaroos bounded for miles along the flooded bank beside us, belly-deep in water, frantic to escape us, too brain-less to head the other way. Packs of dogs barked hysterically at the threat they thought we posed to the shacks they guarded. Swans, dim-witted as kangaroos but infinitely more graceful, indignantly took off in front of us, landed half a mile down-stream, had to take off again, and then a third time, until, exhausted, they eluded our presumed pursuit simply by turning frantically to port and taking refuge among the paddling trees. Families dashed out of homesteads to wave and take photographs as the *Emmy Lou* hooted her response. And all the time there was the thresh-thresh, thresh-thresh of our twin paddle-wheels and the well-oiled beat of the engine that propelled them. Life on the Murray was blissful.

The more so since the chef who prepared my meals – a young, volatile, red-headed Englishman – had previously cooked in the kitchens of the Savoy and saw no reason to lower his standards now that he was working in the galley of a paddle-steamer. In London, I have eaten at the Savoy and the Connaught; in Paris, Rome, New York and Sydney, I have eaten at their equivalents; but never, anywhere, have I eaten food so exquisite as that with which, thrice daily, I gorged myself on the *Emmy Lou*.

At the outskirts of Barham – where the *Emmy Lou* had been built, whence she had departed on her maiden voyage – it soon became apparent that her return was an event. Both banks were lined by townsfolk aiming Polaroids and Instamatics. The bend across which five heavy telephone cables sagged ominously low teemed with children given the morning off from school. The bridge under which we hoped to sail – if the telephone cables hadn't already scuppered us – had become a packed grandstand.

'You touch *one* of our cables,' threatened the Telecom man, 'I'll prosecute.'

'You can't,' retorted the mild, bespectacled Anthony. 'It's your statutory duty not to obstruct the free navigation of this river, and *your* cables *are* obstructing it.'

The Telecom man compromised by lending us two forked poles with which to raise the five long, heavy cables, so that the *Emmy Lou* could sneak under them. Since two men were required to raise each cable, and each of the five cables hung only a foot from its neighbour, this was hardly adequate. But it was all he would do – apart from promising to shoot us if we severed even one of his beloved lines.

'If *you* get under the cables,' promised the Main Roads man, '*I'll* get you under the bridge.'

Thus encouraged, we headed toward the left bank, where the cables, though still far too low, were at their highest, and the crowd of kindergarten children at its thickest. Heavy red-gum branches blocked our way. Reversing determinedly, the *Emmy Lou* snapped them off. Alan, the skipper, and Paul, the engineer – the former from Adelaide, the latter from Sydney – shouted orders and controlled our drift towards the cables with a rope round the trunk of the amputated tree. Chris, the chef, was in the wheel-house, at the helm. John, the purser, and I, and two members of the crew, watched the menacing cables inch relentlessly closer to *Emmy Lou*'s tall iron funnel as the current drove us downstream.

Using the two forked poles, and assorted lengths of wood, we hoisted the first cable over the funnel. Then dashed back to hoist the second. And forward to save the wheel-house (and the chef) from demolition by the first, and back to the third, and forward for the second. The cable went one way, the *Emmy Lou* another, and I – glued to my forked pole, which seemed to be no less glued to the fourth cable – was about to be pitched into the Murray.

'Russ is in trouble,' bellowed Chris, and, abandoning the helm, sped to my aid.

Finally, each cable hung dejectedly astern of both funnel and wheel-house. The kindergarten children cheered shrilly; Chris promptly went back to his galley, to prepare lunch; Alan took the helm; Paul returned to his beloved engine; Anthony, who had watched the entire, perilous exercise with apparent impassivity, polished his spectacles; and the *Emmy Lou* headed backwards, like an infant descending a flight of stairs, toward the bridge.

This had now been raised to its maximum elevation. Even to my inexpert eye, though, it was inches too low. Bum first, we nevertheless crawled toward it. And, paddle-wheels desperately threshing, managed to retreat just as the funnel seemed certain to be toppled, thereby demolishing all the cabins underneath. The hundreds of locals and their children watching from the two unraised flanks of the bridge, longing equally for triumph and disaster, screamed with enthusiasm. But the river was too high, the elevated portion of the bridge too low, the funnel too tall.

We forgot, though, that the Main Roads man had promised that if *we* got ourselves under the cables, *he* would get us under the bridge. A massive block of concrete was the counterbalance that made possible the manual elevation of the bridge. That block now rested on an 8-inch beam of hardwood. The bridge was slightly lowered: the block of concrete was lifted off its hardwood support: the beam was attacked with a power saw: that portion of the beam upon which the concrete block had previously rested was excised: the block was lowered an extra 8 inches, the bridge raised an extra 8 inches: and the *Emmy Lou* was beckoned forward.

Or, rather, backwards. Holding the *Emmy Lou* not quite stationary against the current, Alan allowed her to move almost imperceptibly downstream. Standing on her stern, I watched the bridge loom overhead – and heard the scream of the crowd. With agonising slowness, the funnel top crept toward the girders on the underside of the bridge.

Standing just in front of the funnel, head bent sharply back, Paul stared upwards. 'Come on, come on,' he urged. Trusting him completely, Alan let the *Emmy Lou* slide on. To certain disaster, it seemed to me, and to the hushed crowd above. 'Come on, come on.' And smooth as silk, snug as a finger slipping into a ring, the *Emmy Lou* slid under the bridge.

When her funnel emerged on the downstream side, with a millimetre to spare, the crowd erupted! Hooting triumphantly, the *Emmy Lou* acknowledged its cheers. Anthony, who had risked his boat and his livelihood rather than decline a challenge, smiled modestly and said, 'So we did it!' John changed into a fresh white shirt and his black trousers. And Chris, his chef's cap fecklessly awry, announced, 'Lunch is ready when you are.'

On then toward Swan Hill, stopping just short of the town at the homestead of one of the river's richest properties, Murray Downs. From the river, one approached the house across a large, well-kept garden whose boundary was patrolled by a psychotic-looking emu whose favourite food was probably golf balls. To the left, a peacock and his mate screeched at one another bad-temperedly. The house's architecture was colonial Victorian-Gothic, its mahogany furniture massively Edwardian and its hall-way adorned with large photographs of conceited, thick-necked rams. The whole symbolised rural Australia at its most prosperous.

In so manifestly Anglo-Saxon and man-made an environment, it is easy to forget that the original owners of Murray Downs were ever prepared to defend their domain against the intrusion of uncivilised blacks; that the property was largely cleared of its innumerable trees by Chinese coolies stranded in Victoria after the collapse of the gold-rush; and that the property is rich mainly because it has always been watered by the Murray. During the worst days of the recent drought, for example, its paddocks had so much grass to spare that the company that owns them could purchase sheep from less fortunate farmers for a few cents a head, fatten them, and sell them for as many dollars.

And so to Swan Hill, with its Disneyland colonial settlement and the old paddle-steamer, *Gem* – which was abandoned half a century ago downstream at Mildura, brought to Swan Hill as a tourist attraction, and now houses a restaurant specialising in witchetty-grub soup and yabbies.

Witchetty-grub soup looks like watery porridge, and tastes vaguely like peanut butter; yabbies, a sort of crayfish, are 85 per cent head and tail, 5 per cent repellent yellow gunge, and 10 per cent white, rubbery, almost tasteless flesh. They are con-sidered a great delicacy and, now that the bloody carp have made them even more elusive than Murray cod, are very expensive.

Returning to the *Emmy Lou*, I collected my dilly bag from my cabin, said my good-byes and marched down the river in search of the vessel that was to transport me first to Mildura and then to Wentworth. Her name, I had been told, was *Merrilinda*, her skipper an old-timer called Paddy Hogg.

When I found her, I was less than enchanted. At Jingellic I had quit the river to avoid the fate of the *African Queen*. *Merrilinda* was the *African Queen* – with a cabin, a small wheel-house, a tarpaulin lean-to above the cabin, and astern, a dinghy laden with an upright, 44-gallon drum of fuel. Perhaps, I thought, there are two *Merrilindas*. 'Mr Hogg?' I called.

An Australian version of Humphrey Bogart emerged. 'Mr Braddon?'

I nodded. I have beautiful manners. I was taken inboard and introduced to the crew – Paddy's married daughter, who would do the cooking, and Zena, who would act as mate. They were friendly, but anxious. The cat had run away. I am allergic to cats. I was taken to my accommodation for the next five days – an iron bedstead in the upper lean-to. Zena found the cat. It looked at me with baleful blue eyes, and hid underneath my bed. We set sail, thunderously, the dinghy lumbering in our wake.

What followed was five days of enchantment. The *Merrilinda* was a working boat, as much a part of the Murray as the Murray herself. Paddy had spent his entire life on the river, respected it, loved it, knew everything about it, had skippered every twentieth-century paddle-steamer plying it, and was a fascinating but unobtrusive talker. Paddy's daughter and Zena worshipped him. The cat hated me and avoided me as if I were a rabid dog. And I – who had become accustomed to a chintzy cabin, a uniformed crew, constant service and *haute cuisine* – felt instantly at home; forgot that I was a metropolitan creature; devoured fried eggs and bacon and munched thick ham sandwiches; consumed endless mugs of tea made with river-water that hitherto (accepting the word of ecology experts, who said it was polluted by salination) I had considered lethal; had no need of books or newspapers; had no desire to write; simply watched the magical river glide by, and belonged.

Arrived at Mildura, I had no desire to go ashore, but did so because we weren't due to sail till the following morning. I walked the length and breadth of the town – which, like many such country towns, presumptuously calls itself a city. All its streets were about a mile wide but as devoid of traffic as they were afflicted by signs warning motorists that there was 'No Standing'. Every intersection had its set of traffic *and* pedestrian lights. People waited to cross any road – and grew visibly older – till the light went green and said WALK. Every lawn and garden was being sprayed with Murray water. The gardens were a riot of blooms so colourful they looked artificial. And in one street there were at least a dozen churches. Mildura, I realised sadly, was without sin. Doubtless those who installed all those traffic lights and No Standing signs had abolished it.

Main street, Mildura, with traffic lights and empty streets

On the other hand, I had a superb chocolate malted at a Greek milk bar, a splendid paella for lunch at a Spanish restaurant, and an exotic dinner at a Lebanese establishment. Then spent the night in a hotel packed with screaming octogenarians who had come hundreds of miles by coach specially, if inexplicably, to see Mildura. I was happy, the next morning, to re-embark on the *Merrilinda*. Next stop, Wentworth.

Except that it rained, causing the river to rise even higher and reach farther between the adjacent trees and across the neighbouring land, nothing happened. Nonetheless, I found the journey fascinating. Two stranded goats stood motionless on top of an almost submerged, fallen tree-trunk, ignoring us and one another. An entirely new creek raced some hundreds of yards across a long, thin, low tongue of land around which the river doubled back upon itself. Swinging the *Merrilinda* to port, Paddy entered the creek. A few minutes later, we re-entered the Murray.

'Saved 15 miles,' Paddy commented matter-of-factly.

A second large river butted its way into ours, from the right. 'The Murrumbidgee,' Paddy advised. Later a third large river, yellow rather than brown, spliced itself into ours. 'The Darling,' said Paddy. 'Runs a thousand miles north up into Queensland.'

Aloud, I wondered why, when they merged so evenly, the Darling had become the Murray rather than the other way round – or even something else entirely? Paddy thought it was a silly question. All the same, my so recently empty mind was rapidly filling.

A paddle-steamer leaving the lock at Mildura

One further question still bothered me, however. *Why* was the Murray so afflicted with salination? After all, it was a freshwater river fed only by thawing snow and unpolluted rain. Whence, therefore, came the salt? As always, Paddy had the answer. By installing dams to control the Murray's flow from the mountains to the sea, man had interfered with nature, constipated the river's annual flush and deprived the riparian red-gum forests of their annual essential paddle in a flood.

Thus unflushed, the river grew sour. The red gums failed to regenerate and their numbers dwindled. Yet it was the roots of the red gum that, in bygone years, had absorbed much of the salt that constantly seeped upwards from a layer of sea-water far below. 'Sea-water hundreds of miles *inland*?' I queried. 'All of this,' replied the imperturbable Paddy, raising one hand from the wheel to gesture at the surrounding plains, 'used to be an inland sea. About four hundred million years ago.'

So now, lacking a sufficiency of the red gums' snaggled roots, the banks contained an excess of salt, which the river washed out of them, into herself. Worse, though, the unnatural weight of irrigation water on the top layer of earth, between which and another layer the residue of the vanished sea was sandwiched, compressed the saline filling and forced it upwards. When floods came, and receded, the salt washed into the Murray. Which, by the time it reached South Australia, whose water-supply it was, had become quite unpotable.

An old gum-tree on the banks of the Murray River

Naturally, South Australia protested. To little avail, however. So long as their orchards, vineyards and pasturelands flourished because of irrigation, New South Wales and Victoria remained indifferent to Adelaide's need for drinking-water. The Murray is not merely the source of much of Australia's prodigious rural wealth, she is also a symbol of her opportunist and self-obsessed state governments.

And of her guilt about the treatment of her aborigines. Not far from Wentworth, where I left the *Merrilinda*, Rufus River, fed by nearby Lake Victoria, runs into the Murray. For centuries, aboriginal tribesmen had hunted and lived there. During the 1830s, however, the white overlander, having grazed the upstream plainlands almost to extinction, began to drive his exhausted sheep and cattle down to Rufus River. Alarmed, the black tribesmen attacked them with spears, killing two shepherds, scattering 5000 sheep and putting the surviving whites to flight. Ten well-armed overlanders returned, were confronted by several hundred blacks, killed eight of them, and were forced to withdraw. Between then and the following August, two expeditions were dispatched to punish the tribesmen, and the blacks killed a small number of whites. But the black force retreated before the threat of the second expedition, then dispersed and hid among the reeds that lined the creek. A prolonged fusillade from the vengeful whites killed about 200 of the cowering tribesmen.

Thereafter tuberculosis, apathy and the loss of their traditional hunting-grounds decimated the tribes and destroyed the fabric of their unique society. The odd list-less aboriginal in riverside towns, the occasional shack on the river's bank, is all that is to be seen of them today.

A Post Office van took me most of the way from Wentworth to Rufus River, the Murray to our left, a bleak plain covered in saltbush to our right. Leaving the van, I walked the rest of the way to the creek. It was raining. Lake Victoria has been dammed. Thereby immensely broadened, it has swamped the lake's one time ad jacent forest of gums. It too has become an aquatic Passchendaele. And sitting drenched on a levee beside it, the creek behind me, I found it difficult to envisage either a habitat for which, for once, the aborigines would go to war, or a source of fresh pasture the overlander would want to invade. All I could see was water so leaden it looked almost like ice, the blasted trunks of drowned trees, and dozens of indifferent pelicans.

On, then, into South Australia, and Renmark – whence, thanks to the integrity of past South Australian governments, the Murray is navigable by steamer almost down to the sea.

Having journeyed thus far by canoe, Cessna, glider, mini-paddle-boat and launch, I now boarded what looked like a savagely truncated ocean liner, the *Murray Queen*. Carrying several hundred passengers, it was the brainchild of an immigrant from Holland and was skippered by a tattooed migrant to the Murray from northernmost Queensland. My earlier suspicion that, almost without exception, today's river entrepreneurs come from anywhere but the river had been confirmed.

The Dutchman's story illustrates the best and worst aspects of post-World-War-II life in Australia. He had been a youngster in Rotterdam during the war, and had become a shipwright. Attracted by Australia, as a land of peace, warmth and oppor-tunity, he and his young wife said goodbye to devastated Holland and settled in

Adelaide, where he got a job with the state railways. Because he was not a member of the relevant union, however, and because that union was a closed shop, making membership impossible, he was fired. He found new employment in a boatyard. Then, perceiving the tourist potential of the Murray, he decided to build a river-ship to exploit it. That ship he named the *Murray Explorer*. It proved so successful a venture that he built a second, the *Murray Queen*. He is now a very wealthy man.

My fellow passengers on the *Murray Queen* were not young and had come on her four-day voyage, they said, to learn more of 'Australia's heritage'. This they did by sitting most of the day in her coffee lounge, reading, playing dominoes or Monopoly, and snoozing; the rest of the day eating the sort of meals provided for today's service-men; and the evening attending quite frightful concerts or singsongs. For the more alert, there were also morning sessions of aerobics and evening games of bingo. Blissfully happy though they were – the women to escape their household chores; the retired men not to have to garden – I was quite unable to share the pleasures of their cruise, and spent all my time on deck, surveying the river.

Now that she would soon be heading southwards, the river began to canter, carving her way through would-be impeding hills, so that her bends were flanked by high, sandstone cliffs and her banks were sloping and unflooded. The cliffs, the Dutch commodore explained, had been thrust up from the floor of the inland sea which had existed forty million years ago. *Forty* million, I wondered, or four hundred million, as Paddy had said? Before my time, I decided. And anyway, every Murray story had at least two versions. So I let it be. 'They found a fossilised shark's tooth embedded in the cliff there,' he added.

'No fossilised snakes?' I asked innocently, having been promised millions of the hateful creatures and seen not one. The question bemused him and he declined even to answer it.

As ever, the secretive, modest Murray revealed nothing of the land that stretched to either side of her. But the absence of pumps revealed that South Australians have no need to plunder her waters for irrigation, and an endless variety of attractive holiday homes proved that here at least her serenity was appreciated.

I fled the *Murray Queen* after two days of its cunningly regimented hilarity and took possession of a houseboat – which resembled nothing so much as a floating garage. Appearances were deceptive, though. It had a sun-deck forrard; behind that, a capacious lounge and kitchen; and behind them, on either side of a narrow passage, three cabins, a bathroom and a lavatory. Its engine shoved it along at a breathtaking 4 knots; it was easy to manoeuvre; and – like the *Merrilinda* – it had the supreme virtue of lying low in the water. Like the interior of a Japanese house, the Murray can only be properly appreciated by those who sit on the floor.

The days that followed were a time of almost mindless pleasure (psychiatrists should prescribe the Murray rather than tranquillisers) and I have only a few recollections of incidents. Birds nesting in the sandstone cliffs. No idea what sort. All river-birds are ducks to me. A visit one evening, when I was moored to the bank, by a small angora nanny goat which sniffed at my hand with a velvet nose and stared at me with mad eyes. A vast flock of pelicans roosting on a rare expanse of floodland, who ignored my floating garage completely. Listening to the local radio station, which broadcast nothing but the day's prices for lamb and tomatoes. And my sole – albeit vicarious – encounter with a snake.

Mooring one evening, I talked to a fisherman who was surrounded by the corpses of a dozen murdered carp. 'Shoulda bin here an hour ago,' he advised. 'Snake swam across the river to that lot over there.' That lot over there were a camping family – parents, children and a dog. Observing the snake's hostile approach, the father grabbed his rifle. 'Don't shoot it, don't shoot it,' his idiot children pleaded. 'It's beautiful.' So when it beached, and slithered purposefully toward his loved ones, father nobly pinned its head down with the butt of his rifle, grabbed it by its tail, whirled it in the air, and hurled it 40 yards back into the river.

Whereupon the deadly reptile turned straight round and again headed towards him. His dog fled, his children cowered and his wife screamed. Reaching the bank, the snake reared, hissed and glared at his bare legs.

So he blew its head off.

At which his wife clapped, his children cheered and his heroic dog attacked the serpent's writhing, lifeless trunk and tail. Not as good a story as *my* being bitten, and dying in agony, would have been; but better, after all the promises, than nothing.

And so to Morgan, a pretty little town that was once a thriving railhead where produce was taken from frequent goods trains and loaded on to waiting barges to be towed downstream for sale in Adelaide. Now it is trainless and steamerless and evinces no signs of life whatsoever. Morgan's main claims to fame today are a caravan park for summer tourists, a memorial to the explorer Sturt, and the fact that this is where the Murray finally turns southwards, and changes from a canter to a gallop as she heads for freedom in the sea. Downstream a piece, I sat on a hilltop, gazing at the river far below, and waited for the *Murray Explorer* to round a nearby, cliff-flanked bend.

She appeared abruptly, moving faster than I had expected. Clutching my dilly bag, I sped down the steep side of the hill. Seconds before I reached the bank, the *Explorer* passed me. But its speedboat was waiting for me. Hurling myself aboard, we sped after the Dutchman's senior brainchild.

More aerobics, bingo and concerts. Another full complement of passengers in alleged pursuit of their heritage. Even a fancy-dress ball. Withdrawing misanthropically from their undeniable enjoyment of it all, I spent my last two days on the sports deck, sitting in the rain, assailed by an icy gale, surveying the Murray.

Meantime, and for the first time, the river seemed not only to have lost all character – flanked as it had become by low hills rather than tall trees or cliffs – but also much of its sense of purpose. Someone once told me that, in aboriginal lore, the Murray started life as a snake goddess who, at the very end of her journey, had lost her way. Apocryphal or not, the legend lent a certain metaphorical charm to a vista that had now become bleakly prosaic.

Almost immediately, though, that charming illusion was dispelled as each bank fell sharply aside and the river became a large, featureless lake. If the Murray had once been a divine snake, she must have swallowed an elephant before she expired. To my eye, the lake was as shocking a sight as a goitre on a beautiful woman's once-slender throat. Incisive as a surgeon's knife, however, the *Explorer* sliced through

The Murray River winds through sandbanks into the sea

the goitre; and some hours later the distant banks reconverged. Soon the lake was behind us and we were sailing down a river again, to Goolwa, our last port of call.

Disembarking, my journey almost done, I climbed into a Cessna, to which floats had been attached, and flew a mile or so downstream to witness the Murray's debouch into the sea. How dramatic it would be, I thought; how violently her 1700 miles of flood-water would rupture the last of her terrestrial constraints.

Instead, her energy almost dissipated by the demands of that upstream lake, she trickled wearily between two low sand-spits and was promptly swallowed by an ungrateful ocean that stretches, unbroken, to Antarctica. I could have walked across her, she was so shallow and narrow and puny.

We landed behind the farther spit and waded ashore. The sand, to a depth of several feet, was studded with empty pippi shells – a sure sign that aborigines had once camped there. 'They attacked Sturt's lieutenant here and killed him,' my pilot told me.

I picked up one of the shells and we waded back to the Cessna. That shell is beside me now, reminding me that civilisations come and go but great rivers endure. A hundred years hence, Australia may have become Asian, or Russian, or unequivocally vulgar. Unless we have meanwhile transformed her into a serpent of solid salt, however, the Murray will still be flowing unconcernedly from the mountains to her rendezvous with the indifferent sea.

THE NILE

Brian Thompson

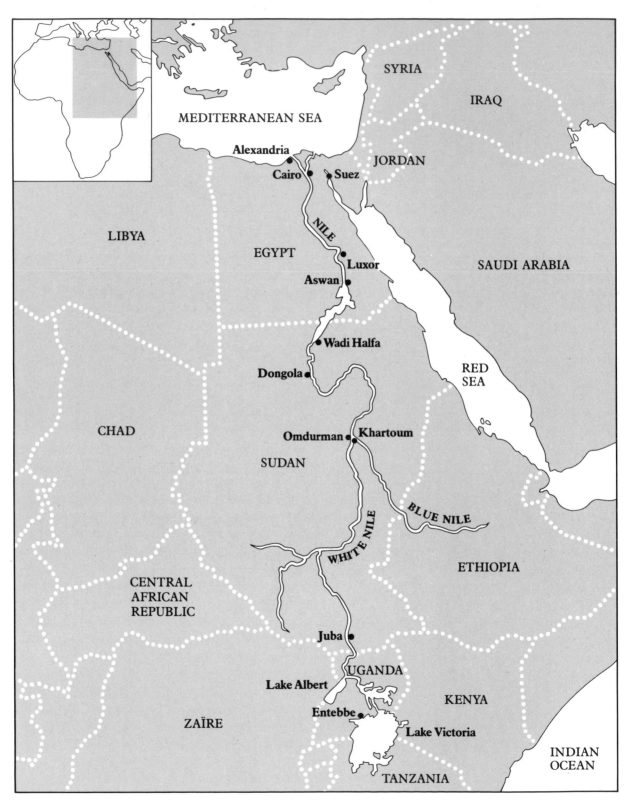

You arrive in Khartoum by air and at night. Above the junction of the Blue and White Niles, the moon hangs like a slice of melon and the stars are as plump and juicy as pomegranate seeds. Out there, you sense, with more than a little apprehension, is a great and dignified emptiness which is in itself a contradiction of the modern age. Out there, in landscapes you have only guessed at from the comforts of the plane, is another scale of existence altogether.

Cairo, where you made your stopover, was hideous with guns and uniforms. Here in Sudan the air is more wistful, as befits the poorer neighbour. Yet in both these cities, despite the noise and confusion of one, and the laconic modesty of the other, there is in the air and in the faces of the people on the street a quality we associate with great antiquity. Even in the first moments of the journey, each of these places seems to exhibit that exquisite sadness we find so fugitive in our own culture. Part of this comes from the proximity of the desert. The moon and stars reflected in the waters of the Nile is an image that predates man and will assuredly outlast him. The moon's glass is a river older than the desert itself. Forests of cedar have become stone and rubble along its banks. Kingdoms have risen to glory and fallen away into dust. The river is unchanging. The arabic name for it is *al bahr*, the sea.

The Nile is so immense and so ancient that a journey down it needs a prologue. In 453 BC, a young Greek historian, Herodotus, penetrated upstream as far as Aswan, where in his time five impassable waterfalls formed the first cataract. He was standing at the limit to Upper Egypt. What lay beyond was a matter of purest conjecture. That there were great kingdoms to the south, such as had provided Solomon his Sheba, was known. But where the river rose was another matter. Herodotus turned his back on the problem. With the perception of an intelligent interloper, he saw that what really counted was that Egypt itself was the gift of this river. The annual Nile flood could be predicted to within a few days and was so reliable that the Ancient Egyptians had founded their calendar on it. Each year, at a time when the rivers of Greece dried up, a tumultuous Nile poured through the cataract from some unimaginable place.

The search for the sources of the Nile is one of the great adventure stories of modern times. It is not yet 125 years since Speke stood in ecstasy at the outflow from Lake Victoria. Even after the source of the White Nile had been discovered there lay between Ripon Falls in Uganda and Aswan in Egypt a huge, incoherent country practically without boundaries, famous only for slaves and gold. For while, in its last 800 miles to the sea, the Nile had created one of the great world civilisations, in its upper reaches there was until within living memory nothing to report but despair, exasperation and dismay. Sudan remains Africa's largest and emptiest country. In contemporary Egypt, you visit a country confused in its loyalties, and strident with politics. In Sudan there is the unanimity of poverty. No two neighbour countries could offer more different experiences.

Nowadays millions make the historical pilgrimage to Egypt. Even the Israelis have a tour provided, which takes in the Russian-built dam at Aswan, along with the reed-banks where Moses was cast out. In the great temples of Luxor and Karnak, no sooner has one guide finished speaking in, say, German, than another takes his place with an identical exposition in French or Italian, Japanese or English. One of the tour operators from England has a guide – a lady – who marches at the head of her troops through all this rabble, holding aloft a pennant in Conservative blue. Two hours here, two hours there, tomorrow the Pyramids. Some of the tourists are genuine amateurs of archaeology and the richness of Egyptian dynastic history. Some are simply bemused. In a place called Kom Ombo I saw a temple being inspected by an Italian woman in white high heels, silver knickers and an otherwise completely see-through jump suit, decorated with tiger stripes. In a corner of this particular temple was a heap of mummified crocodiles, piled up like rolls of lino in an outhouse. The beautiful, scandalous Italian teetered off back down a dusty track, besieged by hawkers trying to sell her tablecloths, the likeness of gods, amulets and scarabs. Strictly speaking, the sight of her was a provocation and a disgrace: but she borrowed a little, perhaps, from Cleopatra. Like that great lady, her river-boat was her refuge. Once on board, she could wash the dust from her feet, and look inwards to a luxury only guessed at from the bank. She might slip on her bikini and sit by the upper-deck pool, change lenses on her camera, and relax, ice tinkling in a Martini at her elbow.

Over 1000 miles to the south, but on the banks of the same river, is a little town called Juba. It is set in the green heart of Africa: to strike out from there in one direction would be to cross the watershed that feeds both the Nile and the Congo. The White Nile runs into the town from Uganda. It is a glassy green ribbon of water, perhaps 30 yards wide, banked by rushes. In the distance are the straw cones of a village. Here, in the foreground, naked boys wade up to their hips in the river, fishing. Their bodies are proportioned like dancers, their skins as black as grapes.

I arrived in March, by courtesy of the Sudanese military, flying down from Khartoum as supercargo on a Hercules C-140. Twice the flight had been delayed. Twice I sat in the fitters' mess, sipping mint tea with the lads, or pacing up and down in the shade of the wing, watching the tarmac sizzle. I landed in Juba at last with the pleasant feeling of having achieved the near impossible. To begin a journey, you must have the excitement of departure. Let me tell you that you get off the plane in Juba into a heat that is almost overwhelming, and you tremble for your temerity. Walking in Juba today, in the twentieth century, when the sky is full of man-made satellites, puts you in a privileged class: there can be few places more securely locked away from the European experience. In the history of the Nile as seen from the Delta, Juba is quite strictly the back of beyond.

The river itself was low – lower than for some years, it was explained. Down by the ramshackle wharf weeds grew through a stack of iron pipes. A couple of decrepit steamers were warped up together, and from the transoms of these boats girls flicked up tins of water on the end of long strings. There was a decided moodiness in the air. Overhead, an uneasy sky brooded. And then, to everyone's surprise, it rained. The cigarette-seller who sat by a rusty meat-safe (his shop) slipped the entire stock into his shirt and scampered off to the cover of some trees. The naked boys ran through the meadows, their fish jiggling on the end of poles.

Juba is a provincial capital. It is laid out in an unmistakable British fashion, in wide avenues of red-washed bungalows, many of them with rusting tin roofs. Red and green are the colours of Juba – red for the roads and the houses, green for the faintly lascivious river and the fronds of plants. There are a few two-storey offices in the government quarter. A girl in a white dress sits under a tree in the compound of such a place. She is knock-kneed and listless, and her eyes are cast down. A dog sprawls in a broken culvert. The clerks who work in the building behind her dress fastidiously in the European style, and are called Matthew or Samuel, Ruth or Rebecca. The unbidden presence in all the compounds, and all the rooms of all the offices, is the heat. A thoroughly African languor hangs over everything. In the offices of the boss, the air-conditioning works in fits and starts. When it comes on, a gale of air blows and riffles the surface of the tea in the cup of the great man. But the machinery may suddenly stop, and then he gets up in exasperation from behind his desk. Juba is the country of Conrad and Greene, without a doubt.

In the Juba Hotel, the grounds are more or less laid out by pavements of up-ended, green beer bottles, their necks sunk into the earth and whimsically hammered home. From the terrace, in the cool of the evening, you can gaze into the flaking excavations of a swimming-pool where the last high dive executed was probably the night before independence in 1956. You drink, you go to your room and collapse on a bed to gaze at the cement ceiling, all in a sort of literary fog, with the uncanny feeling of being written about by someone who fled the same scene a few years ago. One night I walked up the road to the People's Party Park, arriving as the whole town was plunged into blackout. I sat in a rustling darkness, served by girls who were invisible a foot from the table. It is the fashion in the People's Party Park to drink and then hurl the bottle from you like Byron. All round me the empties skittered in the grass, or rang companionably against the legs of a neighbour's table.

'You tell me please,' a voice in the dark asked. 'What is your country and what political opinion do you hold?'

I sketched an answer, to which there was a low musical laugh. 'I think if you are British you are a follower of Mr Enoch Powell.'

'No. Perhaps you can name another British politician?'

This time the laugh was sardonic. Another bottle skipped by.

The river is the way out of Juba. A surprisingly large boat plies between here and Kosti. Once, all this part of Africa was the wrong side of the fearsome Sudd, a vast inland swamp of some quarter of a million square miles. Many princes in history sent messengers to the northern limits of the Sudd, only to have them come back and shake their heads. Until little more than a century ago, the Sudd was as impenetrable an obstacle as existed on the face of the earth, and well within recent memory it was a notorious killer. River-steamers foundered in it, not by sinking, but choking. Like the guests of the Emperor Heliogabalus, who were suffocated when the room filled with rose petals, the old river traffic would sometimes die half laughing, as the lotus and the papyrus engulfed it. These days the government steamer, *Wadi Halfa*, makes the passage in three days, barring accidents, of which as it happens there were several. We ran aground more than once.

The passengers included half a dozen white people who had come further than I, and whose further horizons were unlimited. They were the new tourists, the fancy-free young. The Australian you would expect to meet in such a company turned out to be the beautiful, shy Sue Ellen, who had come in from Kenya after two years on the road, and was half thinking of bending her steps back towards Sydney. There was Tom, from Southern California; Roy from Canada; a Dutch boy and his friend who had been held by the secret police in Uganda; a young student making his way to Oxford six months hence. All of us exclaimed at the comforts of the boat and the wonderful grace of the Dinka people, whose villages and cattle-camps line the banks of the river.

For at this point, before the Sudd begins, the country is at this season of the year dry savannah. The physical beauty of the southern Sudanese, quite as much as the landscape and fauna of this part of the world, has exercised a strange fascination over the European mind. The appeal is romantic and associative: it is, at the heart of it, literary. What we want from these people, if we were able to explain it, would seem to them perhaps the manifestation of a disease. What we expect to find in faraway places is an innocence beyond our powers to create for ourselves in our own place.

Two young girls run down to witness the passing of the boat – its steel, its energy against their nudity. They stand in a posture of concern, almost, their fingers to their

Goats graze in front of round huts in a village near Juba. Right: Dinka tribesman with a long-horned ox. The Dinka cover themselves with ash to help keep off the flies and mosquitoes that plague the Sudd. Far right: a Dinka man wearing a bead necklace which indicates that he is engaged to be married

lips, their weight on one leg, throwing the hip out. They seem like primordial women: and as you lift your glance from them, you see two men, likewise naked, walking briskly away with long strides towards the trees. They are all members of the Dinka Bor, one of the great riverine tribes.

The *Wadi Halfa* ran aground, on a very memorable night, immediately opposite a Dinka cattle-camp. The whole wealth of this tribe is in cattle, and it is left entirely in the charge of children and adolescent boys. They are stark naked, totally unself-conscious, and like no other human beings I have seen. Their bodies are covered in wood-ash to give some protection from mosquito bites, so that in the dawn, as they woke and unpegged the cattle, they were spectral shapes, lit by a magenta sun. But when the rains come, these same children leave the river-camps, for there is water in the hinterland, and once there they put on clothes and go to school.

'You cannot speak about Africa,' Tom from California says, 'until you have experienced the poverty of these people.' And then he adds, with an unconscious ingenuousness, 'Right now there is no place on earth I'd rather be.'

It is easy to understand that remark. The traveller who heads north down the Nile is passing from a mystery towards a more mundane state of affairs. The river lends

this passage a morbid kind of beauty. Hour after hour, once the steamer is in the grip of the Sudd, the horizon is filled with green swamp. Even from the modest elevation of the cabin decks you can see dozens of miles, across mats of lotus and papyrus thick enough to walk on, tenanted only every so often by a family struggling with a dugout canoe against the wake of the ship. It is said that the Nuer have only two points of the compass – west and east, the river and the grazing lands. What's north or south is a matter of indifference. And every time the ship swamped a canoe, or ran a con-temptuous bow-wave along a landing place cut from the reeds, the point was made. We were running against the Nuer way of life, running away from aboriginal sim-plicity. The agents of the Pharaohs reached as far as this, and turned back in disgust. Apart from the beauty of the people, nothing of value existed here.

The shipboard life reminded me a little of the principle of the glass-bottomed boat. We skimmed and goggled. The *Wadi Halfa* makes the passage through the Sudd without stops, for there is nowhere defined enough to be a stopping place. At night, barring the misfortune of running aground, it ploughs steadily onwards, piloted by means of a searchlight playing on the water ahead. There is a steady breeze, ideal for washing clothes. Invited to a meal, Sue Ellen washed all her clothes, shampooed her hair and sat sunburned and patient in the door to her cabin. There was talk among these new tourists of thefts and muggings, internments and beatings. One of the travellers was an amazingly beautiful Kampuchean girl, too shy to appear on deck. Of the Sudanese, the bulkiest and most genial turned out to be a colonel in mufti.

'Well now, you see down there in the south we have some oil. This will make a big difference.'

'But I have heard that the oil will cause a great many political problems for you?'

He laughed: 'Actually it is no more than 30,000 barrels a day. But the real answer to your question is that Sudan is one nation and one people.'

'With eight international boundaries.'

'Yes, that's so. And I don't know how many languages.' His laugh boomed down the deck.

At Malakal, the clear-water Nile resumes and at once the atmosphere is different. The light seems to have altered, the quays are piled high with sacks, the police trucks seem smarter and more purposeful. The green of the Sudd has disappeared, and flying over the town is the green flag of Islam. It is altogether a sharper green.

In 1881 a holy man arose from contemplation on an island in the middle of the Nile below Malakal and declared himself the Mahdi, the Expected One, whose coming was presaged by the Prophet, and whose duty was to bring about the end of the world by destruction so that something better might arise in its place. For four years there raged a disastrous civil war in which it is said half the population perished. In the course of the tumult Gordon was murdered and the Mahdi himself died, of a fever. A conclusion to matters was later forced by the icy heart and brain of Kitchener, at the Mahdi's headquarters, Omdurman, in 1898.

Cromer called Omdurman the 'filthy capital of Mahdi-ism'. The ramparts of the old dervish forts are still to be seen. They overlook a placid beach where now the trucks and lorries of Khartoum go down to be washed. Within these walls of mud, on

The Mahdi's tomb at Omdurman

a particular September morning, 17,000 of the faithful perished under Kitchener's artillery and Maxim guns. Kitchener himself steamed past the carnage and turned into the Blue Nile, where he reoccupied the Governor's Palace. Under his direction, Khartoum was laid out in the shape of a Union Jack; as for the Mahdi, his tomb was broken open and the bones of the imam flung into the Nile. With peculiar crassness, Kitchener had the skull sent down to Cairo with the intention of having it made into an inkstand for Queen Victoria. (The horrified staff returned it, and it came back up-river as far as Wadi Halfa.) But the Sudanese have a proverb: he who dies in the river returns a giant. Today the monstrous personality of Kitchener is extinguished from Sudanese history. Khartoum and Omdurman dwell together on opposing banks of the river. As a sort of emblem of such dark episodes, the two Niles meet and remain for a mile or so sharply distinct colours. At the very junction there is a People's Palace, erected by the Chinese.

I expected Khartoum to be a forest of masts. Nothing could be further from the truth. The great topic of conversation here is petrol. At the time the queue for petrol was three days long, and for diesel as much as seventeen days. There is a shortage of practically everything in Khartoum, for all that it is the industrial base of the country. You quite quickly grasp that you are in a capital city of a country held together by political rhetoric, foreign aid and a desert-bred fortitude. At nightfall, as the trucks and cabs limp past and the dusty neon lights are switched on here and there, you have the uneasy feeling that it is quite within the bounds of possibility for you to wake tomorrow and discover everyone in the city has gone – given up and turned away from the twentieth century with a rueful smile.

'You know,' an old man said to me as we talked in a colonnade of trees laid out beside the river, 'our country is the biggest producer in the world of donkey clover. One day, therefore, when you in Europe return to riding on donkeys, we shall be a very rich nation.'

It was a joke that sat well with the laconic dignity and beauty of the Sudanese, who must be among the nicest people in the world. In the international airport, with its ramshackle accommodation, a young man has scratched into the table-top: 'Fare-well, beloved Sudan! From your devoted son, Abdullah.' His destination was most likely some shanty town, and he left behind a city of a million people never seen by the outsider's eye as truly belonging. To be sure there are men in suits and girls in blouses and miniskirts. There are shops selling what seem like impossible luxuries, such as video cameras. But on the southern side of the city is a vast souk beside a bus depot, where thousands of people seem to be getting out, going home. To the north, the way the river runs, these buses suddenly veer off the road and plunge into the desert as surely as a boat launched into the ocean from a Pacific atoll. In the flying dust and teeth-rattling emptiness, Khartoum seems to dwindle like a half-forgotten dream.

For nobody leaves by boat. A little below Khartoum is the sixth cataract – numbering from Egypt. To descend the Nile through these six cataracts is not possible. Kitchener reconquered the Sudan by the expediency of a railway, which cut across the great ox-bow the river makes as it hits the basalt of the Nubian Desert. The Arabs call this region the Belly of Stones. After Atbara, where the last of the Nile tributaries comes in, the river is turned west and even south for a while before finding its way back. It is here that you can pick up stone that was once wood, in the days when this barren country was an abundant forest. Maps of the region are forebodingly empty, and while the desert is amazingly beautiful, even colourful, its antiquity is prodding a strange nerve. At night you lie under the stars, your back to one eternity, gazing up into another. All around you is the gouged-out emptiness of millennia. There is a story told of the engineers who brought Kitchener's railway from Egypt. They were startled to find tribesmen in full armour, probably looted from the Crusades. For the horsemen, however, inured to a time-scale dictated by the desert, the acquisition of the armour was but a moment ago. So it is when you stumble through the Roman ruins below Shendi, or the vast crockery tip of the temple at Dubishaya, where shards of pottery 2000 years old are swept up in huge heaps. You feel, even as a casual visitor to the desert, a sense of historical indifference.

But while you cannot travel the whole way to Egypt by boat, you can take a three-day voyage round the loop of the Nile, starting at a place called Karima. It is a rail-head that abuts a boatyard of hulks, one of which turned out to be the mail-boat *Kerbekan*. I happened to be twelve hours early for embarkation, much to the indignation of the official in charge. After some confusion, and watched by the crew, who were taking their ease under a tree, I was waved on board. The vessel was completely deserted and remained so all the hours of daylight. In the bows, on the first-class deck, a wire mesh screened the deck lounge, once peopled by long-forgotten District Officers and their wives. There were one or two other touches of a disavowed past: the *Kerbekan* had a little of Henley about it, for all its dilapidation. I fondly imagined it to be a hundred years old at least: it was actually put into service in 1948, yet seemed to have been painted and furnished by ambitious art directors. It needed only Lee Marvin at the helm to be straight from the silver screen. The cabins were grubby, the fans thick with flies, everything about it was a cause for dismay – and I fell in love with it immediately. The only thing to drink was water from the Nile, laced with sterilising tablets. The only other passengers on board were the cockroaches.

Then, during the night, the *Kerbekan* cranked up its Gardner engines, lashed a couple of barges to itself and set off at a juddering waddle. Like a good ship anywhere, once under way it came to life, and exhibited as much personality as any movie star. For three days and nights there was never a moment between us that wasn't love. It began at breakfast, when the steward flung a bed-sheet over the rickety table, produced from the folds of his robe salt and pepper in a rusty sardine tin, and then, triumphantly, served egg and chips. Is there anything better to do in life than sail down the broad and placid Nile, in the very heart of nowhere, eating such a gourmet dish, and talking in signs and broken English to the cook, who had the recipe of his former employers, the Sergeants' Mess, RAF Wadi Halfa?

The postmaster of the vessel was the plump and energetic Mr Abbas, who spoke good English (although he had not been taught it for thirty years) and insisted on instructing me in Arabic. His assistants found this a matter of amusement. We drank the sweet tea of the Sudan sent in by the cook as he pointed to this and that, barking out its name. The post-room was at the very stern of the boat, just above the water-line, and next door to the mighty Gardners. Every hour or so, the boat would put in at some particular patch of sand. Then the engines would change their rhythm and send the whole deck vibrating. Never a town that one could see – not so much as a hut – but there on the bank would be waiting a great crowd of people. At one place I watched a young soldier land, carrying on his head a plastic table and four chairs. His wife was waiting in the shade of a palm, half-way up the steep bank. She was exquisitely beautiful and composed, dressed in a mauve *tobh* that clung to her in the desert breeze. She, the husband and the furniture arranged themselves in a tiny skiff, and the soldier rowed them on the current to the opposite bank, where the in-laws waited, seemingly suspended in mid-air by the heat mirage.

'That is very beautiful,' I said to Mr Abbas. He replied gravely by giving me the names for table and chair.

'Tell me,' a young teacher asked, 'what do you think of that girl?'

'The woman in the boat?'

'No. No. *That* one.' He pointed shamelessly to a young schoolgirl idly chewing a twig.

'Very beautiful.'

'Yes! She has stolen the sleep from my eyes.'

'Indeed?'

'Completely.'

'What is her name?'

'How should I know that?'

The captain of the *Kerbekan* is above the immediate concerns of his passengers. It is said that the only good river pilots are those from Dongola, for which we were bound. He sat in a brown robe and scarf, gazing sternly on the water which was unaccountably low. When he caught my eye he raised his hand to his forehead in a grave but warning salute. Mr Abbas told me, in one of his excellent excursions into allusion, that the *Kerbekan* was no less than the Queen Mother of the river fleet, and we did indeed sail on the stream with gracious majesty.

At dusk the river turned to wine. In the dawn it was overlaid with pearl, which slowly dissolved to a delicate green, banked by sands that in some places ran down into the water, and in others were held back a foot or so by blackened cliffs. On one side of the ship you looked at the landscape across one of the barges which accompanied us and was set aside for women. On the other side, the men's barge. They slept and ate on deck. A boy of about seven came to me and asked if I knew Bradford.

'Yes, I know Bradford well.'

He shrugged expressively. 'My brother is in Bradford,' he said, and wrote down the last address the family had from him. It turned out his sister was the beautiful girl who had stolen sleep from the schoolteacher's eyes. But on the second morning their space on the deck was empty. Before I rose, they had disembarked at some scrap of beach and simply melted away into the desert.

'Where have they gone?' I asked the schoolteacher. He shook his head. 'She was not so lovely as I thought. Anyway, I can't afford her. You tell me: who is your favourite film star?'

'You tell me yours first.'

'Clint Eastwood,' he said with a bit of a smirk.

All this stretch of the Nile has a dynastic history attached to it. It has been forgotten by all but scholars. In the last days of the Egyptian Empire, the Meroetic kingdoms did try their strength against their northern enemies, who had for so long pillaged Nubia for gold and slaves. There are rocks set in the Nile which bear bombastic inscriptions: *You people from the south, this far and no further*. At the heyday of Egyptian civilisation it was only the cataracts that prevented the extension of the empire southwards. As it was, the Pharaoh's agents scoured this land for slaves and gold and then retreated. They seem to have kept scant records of what they found below Aswan – the people, the temples, the way of life – and what remains today is confusing to the traveller. But between Karima and Dongola it is possible to travel the Nile and hardly look out at its banks, exchanging the sense of motion for a feeling of community. It is typical of Sudan that Karima is hard to get to, and Dongola hard to leave; but these two towns and the boat that connects them are as much as anyone could wish for in the way of human fascination. The three days' jaunt on the river is hard won. Neither Karima nor Dongola have what is called European accommodation, and you would be nicely described as being in the middle of nowhere at any point between the two. But if you like people, and can endure hot countries, this is one of the last adventures to be had on the Nile.

The river is wide, and quite fittingly empty. There is nothing to be seen along its banks, for the sand has been ridged by the wind to make a wavy dune a few feet high. Here and there a cliff rises above the sand; the stone is blackened by the sun. The mood of the Nile, in this desperate place, is nevertheless gentle. Its gender is feminine. The very term *eau de nil*, as a description of a colour, finds its origin here: the best medium in which to paint would be water-colour. Green, silver, lavender; the sand sometimes a dark orange, sometimes bleached almost white; and a vast, overarching sky. From time to time small islands of sand appear in the stream – islands without a scrap of vegetation that are made of silt sent down by the Blue Nile and rolled this way and that through the millennia. To travel this stretch of the river is to cherish silence.

All the same, what was untouchable in the south (as if by touching you would contaminate the object of your desire) is in the north there to be shared. I landed in Dongola as though the place were a vast city. It most certainly isn't that, but the desert teaches you to make the most of a congregation. The trusty old *Kerbekan* staggered to a halt by a pan of silt, that soon rose in clouds about it. After so much solitude, we were a bit like the tightrope walker who skips the last few paces to the safety of his platform. We said our goodbyes in a spirit of excitement.

I was picked up by a friendly cab-driver. I asked him whether there was a place which sold European pipe-tobacco. His eyes widened as he tried to stop himself from fainting with internal laughter. Well, I thought, this was a provincial capital – indeed, the place that had given us the president of the country – so, I said, was there at any rate a hotel? We drove through some miserable streets that gave off the un-mistakable air of early closing, and fetched up at a grimy, two-storey building. It was an Arab hotel where the kitchen staff were vengefully slinging pots and pans about at the end of some intertribal squabble. There were not rooms to be had, but beds in dormitories. The smallest of these contained four beds, the mattresses moulded to the dreams of whole generations of sleepers. The cab-driver began to sense my dismay. The scrambled eggs I ordered were knocked up in the same oil as was used for the fish, the staple of Dongolese cuisine. The driver pointed this out. Wouldn't I rather have some fish? I explained that I had set my heart on eggs. Did he know what an omelette was?

Well, he didn't, but recognising that he had a crazy man on his hands, he drove me to his mother's place, a mud house at the edge of the desert. She came out and gave me the once-over with a mother's shrewdness, and then made, so far as I can judge, the first omelette ever whipped up in those parts.

The principal lesson a European can learn from hot countries is the way they wreck his scale of time. How absurd, looking back on it, this petulant desire for shaving water, omelettes, single rooms, and all the rest of it. But the truth is that they are not so much material comforts, or the expression of customary habit, as ways of measuring the time in a familiar way. In the heart of the desert near Shendi I had come across some American matrons in a truck who had brought with them not only plenty to drink, but enough bottled mineral water to bathe in. They did just that, standing on towels in the moonlight, pouring mineral water over each other, and watched (although they did not know it) by some herdsmen who walked half a day to fetch *their* water from a distant well.

I don't think indignation is the right response. Travel alters clocks: it alters *all* the clocks by which we understand our lives. It is the first real breakthrough in a long journey when you can sit and be patient. I had an opportunity to practise this when I went to the Provincial Governor's residence to make a phone call. The telephone equipment had been put in by Standard Telephones, who might be surprised to hear how skilful birds are at nesting in parts of their hardware. I sat in the post and telegraph room looking out on the ruination of a garden, while as many as five people had a go at making the handset work. Some favoured banging it on the desk, as if exterminating a killer tortoise, some were for turning the thing upside-down. More tea was sent for. A man arrived by motor-cycle whom at first I took to be a high official. He was just a passer-by. In the corner an old man tapped out messages on a telegraphist's key that might have been there in Kitchener's day.

You cannot deride it, any more than you can be angry with the American women giggling naked in the moonlight. For on the whole hot countries are poor countries, and peasant countries: who cares about a telephone call? In Africa, Sudan is among the poorest of all. But I never expect to be among more generous and likeable people. The man who wrote on the airport table, 'Farewell, beloved Sudan!' knew what he was talking about. It is a country inviting love, and deserving respect.

The present-day boundary between Sudan and Egypt is drawn across Lake Nasser, a vast sheet of water formed from the backing up of the Nile by the High Dam at Aswan. In the context of this particular journey, it is the ruthless interposition of modern times with a vengeance. A whole people and its culture were uprooted by the flooding of the Nubian Nile Valley. You cross on a ferry that is electric with tension and anxiety, for most of the passengers are going to look for work and a new life. There is nothing glamorous about this boat, which is, after three or four days of passage, filthy and dismal. Your first sight of Egypt is the dam itself, and you dock

Sudan: fishing-boats at the shore of the Nile

under the eyes of the police, the customs, and the ubiquitous secret police. You are in another dimension altogether.

The strange thing about Egypt is that it manages to be a vast museum and an underground bomb silo all at the same time. There is a much greater volatility apparent: things are more strident, noisier and fuller with apprehension. It is said that as much remains buried from Pharaonic times as has been dug up; and you sense, too, that much of the billion dollars a year the Egyptians receive in American aid is likewise underneath the sand, in the form of rockets and weapon stores. So it is that you explore Egypt walking, as it were, on eggshells.

Aswan is one of those places in the world that has a zero rainfall. All its water comes from the Nile. The cataracts that Herodotus clambered over have all but disappeared. and the river runs through the town as placidly as the Thames at Windsor.

'You sail very well,' I said to the boatman on my first felucca ride. He shrugged. 'Some foreigners can also sail. Did you know David Niven? He liked to sail this boat.'

The film *Death on the Nile* is a re-creation of a vanished Aswan. Today the tour boats are miniature look-alike hotels, and the tourists not at all the classy folk depicted by Agatha Christie. In the old days, Aswan was the place to go for part of the year

A street scene from a village near Luxor

when it was cold and wet in Cairo. Nowadays it is more chic to go to the Mediterranean. The first Egyptian television I saw was on a boat moored in Aswan. It was an over-long and sycophantic interview with Marcello Mastroianni. The strange disparity of experience between those who had crossed Lake Nasser and those who lolled on the sun-deck of the cruise boat, waiting for the holiday of a lifetime to begin, was some-how reinforced by the television flickering away in the air-cooled lounge, while servants slipped past with trays of drinks and the steward bells rang in every room. Yet one has to be careful, too, not to disparage. After a trip through the Sudan Nile, there is nothing like sitting under the shower in a pool of red dust, your clothes heaped up for collection by the laundry, sipping iced beer and listening to the air-conditioning. Nor is there any shame in having spent a great deal of money in wishing to rediscover Egyptian antiquity. Rather the reverse. To be sure, the only Egyptian on the cruise was a Coptic doctor, honeymooning with his stunning wife. But the passengers who assembled at Aswan for the cruise to Luxor were very earnestly aware that they were about to take a trip through the world's greatest open-air museum.

The first Europeans to come as far as this were the soldiers of Napoleon. It is said that when they rounded a bend in the river and saw the ruins of Luxor and Karnak, without a word being spoken these grizzled veterans threw their arms to the ground and burst into spontaneous applause. And then the bands formed up and the heroes of a revolution dedicated to the people made a general salute to the greatest continuous autocracy the world has ever seen. I set off from Aswan with this anecdote rattling in my head.

The thirty-two dynasties of Egypt extend over 4000 years. The Nile created, between two deserts and bounded by two seas, a narrow oasis some 800 miles long. The cultivatable soil – the silt of the annual flood – was sometimes a few metres wide, sometimes impressive acres. Every single scrap of it went under the plough. A country that was so rich, compared with its encroaching deserts, was also comparatively hidden away. It was invaded and reinvaded, racked by civil war; it even sent out expeditions of its own from time to time. But the essential Egypt was quite literally on the banks of the river. The temples and tombs speak with a grandiloquence of that Egypt: and above all of the imperative necessity of carrying over all that good fortune into the next life. The colossal architecture of the Pharaohs has its exact rebuttal in the story of Christ's departure from the tomb. When the Christian God is taken down from the cross and immured, his disciples are immediately shown that the physical presence of the body is not necessary to the continuation of the spirit. What you are looking at in the journey to Luxor is the most monumental contrary belief.

We were a strange set of temple-bashers. Some of us found the sites genuinely inspiriting. Some of us, like Herodotus in his day, found them disconcerting. The boat provided guides, of whom Mr Assem was mine. He maintained a rather pained expression in the face of our idle questions. Who had defaced the temple sculptures of Kom Ombo? The Christians, he explained. And who had lived in them when the sand was 10 feet from the roof and blackened the ceilings with their cooking fires? The Christians. Was it not more likely that some tribe of goat-herders had done this? Mr Assem shook his head. This was not possible.

His view of the Egyptian dynasties was intensely nationalistic. There was the true temple style of decoration and the later Roman and Greek variants, by no means as pure. He pointed to the swag of a belly over a kilt cut into the wall. 'Here, as I am explaining, you see the later style. Which is coarser, don't you think?'

Nobody seemed to agree. In our party there was a scepticism. Mr Assem gave a rueful smile. 'Well,' he said. 'I can assure you it is so. You will see the difference when we come to Luxor.'

What was much more apparent to me, his worst pupil, was that for four millennia the architecture and decoration of the temples was consistent and unchanging, considering the means of construction and the labour employed. I was one of those very much not inspired by the ruins, which bespoke a ruthlessness and autocracy almost impossible to conceive. I found myself, in the midst of luxury and well-being, growing very gloomy – and feeling at the same time some shame in that, because others had spent so much in making the pilgrimage. The wonder of Egypt was in the excavation of it. Once revealed, even at the heat of noon, there was a chill about it all that I could not shake off.

The showpiece of the tour companies is Luxor, which was, for 1000 years or more, the greatest city in the world, the much-fabled Thebes of Mediterranean history. On the east bank are the two mighty temples of Luxor and Karnak. Across the river, beyond the few miles of silt, are the dry valleys in which the kings of Egypt had their tombs, and where in 1922 Howard Carter made his sensational discovery of Tutankhamun. Just as Abydos was the place of pilgrimage for ancient Egypt, so it is that this spot is a place which people from all over the world wish to see before they die. It is a very strange feeling to stand witness with them, in front of beautifully preserved friezes and columns. The scale of building in this one city is quite staggering: the human figure is quite overwhelmed. In the temple at Luxor a mosque was built at some time among the roof-beams, at a time before the place was excavated of sand. Now, after the original floor-level is restored, this mosque perches high overhead, no more consequential than a bird's nest.

You make your way round this city despairing of an adequate supply of superlatives. Even for people who have hung 30,000 feet or more above the earth, in company with 400 others, destroying the geography of the ancient world in a jumbo jet, there is something more wonderful about these ruins than the journey they have made to see them. I doubt if many leave again with a larger understanding of the myths and legends depicted on the walls and inscribed on every column. All day long they trudge through dust as fine as talcum powder, their necks craned, their imaginations faltering. There is magnificence here, bearing in mind that all that remains on view are the empty houses of the king-gods. It was not until I returned to England that I found photographs of many of the objects carried away out of Luxor, out of Egypt altogether, in that first craze of excitement. And only then did I see that there was a naturalistic Egyptian art, able to convey the way a fabric stretches a little over a hip, or how a face might look in semi-serious repose.

Thebes flourished when the recorded history of Egypt was already 2000 years old. The city became the repository for all politics, art and religion under the protection of the god Amon. Directed by the priests, this local fertility god became Lord of all Gods and the Creator of the Universe. His most enthusiastic follower was Rameses II, who did not scruple to adopt his likeness. The Ramesseum at Luxor, with its great avenue of sculptures, leads to a hypostyle temple hall 330 feet long and 170 feet wide, the roof supported on immense columns towering into the sky. However serene they appear today, they are witness to a single-minded ferocity that is terrifying.

It is only when you cross the river to the parched valleys in which the kings and queens of Egypt had their tombs that something like a human scale returns – and that because of the purpose for which the places were first built, and then hidden. Those who worked on the elaborate preparations for the royal tombs were afterwards killed. All the same, not one of the tombs that has been discovered shows signs of having remained intact. Quite apart from the sudden interest that comes from seeing where the monsters who dominated the eighteenth and nineteenth dynasties ended up, there are, too, the inhabitant ghosts of the grave-robbers, who in every case overcame the most elaborate deceptions and concealments.

I ought to offer apology, I suppose. Not until long after I came home did I begin to see all these things in a calm light. I arrived in Thebes unprepared and in a sense

Lotus and papyrus columns at Karnak

from the wrong direction, as a traveller from the south. It was somehow extremely disconcerting to be attending these ancient courts in the company of born-again Christians, Israeli beauties, Japanese Shintoists, Swedish socialists. The one story which Mr Assem told us that sticks in my mind is that of the interconnection between the lotus and Ra. Some said in those fearful, cruel days, that when the lotus blossomed, the god Ra was discovered on the calix. But another version of the myth was that when the flower opened, a scarab beetle was revealed. That beetle was changed into a boy, who wept, and whose tears became mankind. When he had given this alternative version, the guide cocked his head in a characteristic eloquence.

'It is all based on such terrible cruelties,' I said as we walked back through the powdery dust.

'Yes,' Mr Assem said gently. 'But I think you may be missing the point.'

From him, the loyal servant of a state not yet thirty years old, the President of which had been assassinated but a few months earlier, it was his sharpest rebuke. The Egypt that had educated him, and put him into the tourist industry, filling his head with antiquity, was somehow all of a piece with the story of Thebes. A country founded in the ruins of an almighty empire lasting 4000 years cannot disavow it.

The decorated tomb of Senedjem

Characteristically, the modern visitor flies back to Cairo. There were other great palace-cities of ancient Egypt: Cairo has little connection with any of them. The Pyramids on its outskirts, the great Step Pyramid of Saqqara only a few miles distant, with its immense avenue leading across the river to Memphis, Cairo is by comparison a modern city. As it stands today, it might be that, in its public squalor, overcrowding, explosive volatility, it is the ultramodern city. The most fervent Cairene could not call it beautiful.

The Nile comes into Cairo tamed, ambling as grey and murky as the Thames through London. Its banks used to be lined with houseboats: not any longer. I watched it from the fifth floor of the Hilton, a stone lighter in weight and disconcertingly scruffy. I was back in a society where casual clothes cost as much as or more than suits, and looking like a million dollars is only partly a metaphor for good health. I emptied out my travel-weary holdall and sent all the clothes to the laundry with a silent apology to the laundry-workers. Then I sat on the floor and tried to sort out the accidental from the necessary. Some shampoo from Luxor had mixed with the tetramycin from London, and glued itself to letters and press passes. There were stones from the desert and pieces of pottery from the forgotten Meroetic temples

The Nile from the Cairo Tower

195

below the third cataract. There was the torch with which I had illuminated the desert fox in Shendi and the water-sterilising tablets with which I had sweetened the Nile in this place and that. There was the book on the Etruscans which had stood gallant service as a sleeping-draught.

Beneath me, in screaming traffic five lanes wide, a man rode a camel over the bridge. He was headed towards the Nasser Tower, or maybe the Western Desert, or maybe just a roadside attraction. The biggest city in Africa, one of the biggest in the world, and the greatest single congregation of Muslims on earth, Cairo bulges at the waistband like a prosperous peasant. On the east side, the hills from which the city was quarried bristle with radio masts and radar scanners, and overlook a massive, turbulent and frenzied mishmash of ideas. The streets are filled with armed soldiers and there are huge portraits of political heroes. A taxi-driver pointed one out.

'This one is a very ignorant man.'

'Who is he?'

'Minister of Culture,' he said cheerfully.

The political centre of the city is probably up by the Al Azhar mosque, which faces the world's earliest university, and where a short walk can lead you back into medieval streets and city gates. But for all the power and politics flowing through this city the outward atmosphere is curiously apolitical and mute. The city motto should be *If he won't do it, I will*. They turn a fast buck in Cairo. I had occasion to look for an address a little way off the tourist map. The cabbie was floundering. Another taxi screamed to a halt.

'Yes, you! Where you want to go? American? Italian?'

The two cabbies then fell into a violent argument in Arabic, louder and louder. The new arrival seized my arm.

'You come with me. I give you better service.'

'Do you know where I want to go?'

'Doesn't matter. Don't pay this man. He's no good.'

'But neither are you if you can't find the way.'

'I'm better,' he insisted.

The Cairo Museum is fittingly a great treasure-house of that Egypt which once belonged to the Pharaohs; but in the streets the references to the past are whimsical and absent-minded. There is the restless, careless quality of a great seaport, without being anywhere near the sea. Is it therefore Mediterranean, as its rich would dearly love it to be thought? Or is it a desert city? Is it a repository of a rich and glittering past? Or is it modern, in the sense that it can sit at the table of the mighty? Its newspapers are printed in French, English and Arabic. You get the impression that half the messages coming in by cable or phone are in code, that every second person you meet has at least some functional connection with the military or secret police. And yet, for all that, the rumbling bass note of the city is still the bazaar.

'You have come in for some medicaments,' a pharmacist whispered hypnotically. 'You see, I am sending out for some mint tea, very good for the stomach. But now, I wish to show you some scents and perfumes, and in this jar, very old, mixture which you add to the drink of your loved one, for greater passion.'

In the end we compromised on a leather wallet and a travelling-bag.

Left: the *Wadi Halfa* on the Nile between Juba and the Sudd. Right: cattle on the banks of the Nile near Khartoum

The *Kerbekan* with two barges at Karima

The banks of the Nile near Dongola

A ferry unloading at Aswan. Brian Thompson is in the centre of the picture

Tribesmen on the banks of the Nile

A pot-well, an ancient but still common means of irrigation. Overleaf: City of the Dead, Cairo

'I make you this price,' he said, with some of Mr Assem's gravity, 'because you are my brother.'

'Yet my brother might make me a free gift of it,' I countered.

'No! This is not the way of brothers. You are an intelligent man. Would you kill a brother? Would you take the bread from a brother's mouth?'

'Well, I will give these things to my loved one.'

'They will give her joy,' he murmured diplomatically. 'But not so great as your return.'

The city is drunk on petrol. Right outside the Cairo Museum is a ramshackle circular walkway the least Pharaoh would have had torn down as an offence to his sight. It enables people to get across the road to a bus-station. Without it, a pedestrian might well die of exposure. Day and night the cars and trucks race through the city in a frenzy. I met a man who can buy a Peugeot at a country auction in Belgium, drive it to Naples, ship it to Alexandria, drive the desert road to Cairo and still come out with a profit. It is the way he makes his living.

It is said that Cairo was founded when a general set his tents there and went on down the Nile to Alexandria, to threaten the Coptic Christians there. When he returned, a pigeon had taken nest in his camp and he there and then decided it was a favourable omen. At times, Cairo can seem like a city created from a pigeon's point of view – lusty, flea-ridden, makeshift and yet full of pickings. Behind the Citadel is the City of the Dead, where huge numbers of people live in the mausoleums of the long departed, camping permanently, like pigeons, in the weathered stones of an area not able to be built on, and strictly off limits to the tourist. The place has the eerie feel of a walled ghetto. Hundreds of tombs are divided into lots, and streets. Some of them are protected by magnificent doors, weathered by centuries. Some are clearly very old indeed. And in them, and among them, live the unofficial poor. I found one family living in an upturned packing-case. In another place a vendor of kosheri, which is a staple of the poorest of the poor, gave me a Cairene's sardonic smile. Above his head, surrealistically, a portable television was showing a performance of *Swan Lake*.

How is a traveller to interpret all this? He exasperates his hosts in one of two ways: by his indignation, or his indifference. And always there is the tourist Cairo, beckoning.

'Have you been to the Pyramids?' an Englishman asked me.

'No.'

'When are you going?'

'I'm not going.'

'Let me get this straight. You're in Egypt, you're making a journey which you'll put on record, and you have no intention of going to Giza? Is that it?'

'Yes.'

'Then you're a bloody fool.'

Just below the Al Azhar mosque is a narrow alley, in which you find the El Fashawi coffee-house. It was founded a couple of years before American Independence, and has remained in the same family ever since. Of the two members of the family who own it now, one is a colonel in the Army, the other a professor of economics. Each time a regime has commenced, the patron has added a huge mirror, imported from France, and these loom over the customers in fly-blown grandeur. The café has only

An Egyptian in his bazaar stall waits for custom

closed its doors once, in the time of Napoleon. The French ordered the owners to serve wine and spirits, and rather than comply, they closed. It was a short inter-regnum. The political and literary history of Egypt has been hatched here in a street café which is certainly no tourist's idea of a night out. Once, the shops and workshops round about would stay open half the night, but by order of the President, the quarter goes dark in the early evening, save for the coffee-shops. I would recommend the Fashawi above the Pyramids for some hint of the extraordinary life Egypt has had since extirpating the French and, little by little, wresting itself from the dying embrace of the Turks.

Nowhere in its length is the generosity of the Nile more ironically marked than in Cairo. Without the river, the whole country would be just another wadi. There are pleasure-boats to be had, and the most chic thing to do is to water-ski past the *two* Hiltons. There are coxed fours and feluccas, speedboats and the groaning barges of river traffic. But the last place you would go to sightsee in this amazing city is the river. A mile or so above the water-skiers, acacia-built barges unload limestone on a mud wharf overlooked by an immense barracks. A few miles below, and the river is preparing to make its last magical gesture. It is getting ready to disappear.

A tea-house in Old Cairo

The Delta is one of the most intensely farmed and productive patches of ground on earth. The Nile's last surprise is its best. From being an ambling, mysterious giant, imperturbable and indifferent, it divides itself into penny packets. As a river, it is now everywhere, cranked up by children from a ditch into their fathers' fields, used, abused, ignored. The last beneficiaries of the river, the fellahin of the Delta, may only hear of what a desert is from the Bedouin who come to graze their sheep on the stubble. They break their backs over the deep, luscious silt the river has fetched down for millennia, and watered by flood without fail. In the heart of the Delta, with pigeons wheeling over the green fields, you are lucky to have seen the Nile in its magnificence – unless you reason that this is it, here under your feet, where the lightest bird leaves its claw-mark in the yielding earth.

All through the region foreigners are instructed by the military not to leave the road, but I was able to visit a village set deep in the flat, green landscape, where standing on a roof gives you another 5 miles of horizon. A wall-eyed man invited us in for tea, and we sat in the courtyard on mats, brushing away the chickens. He was one who had worked in Saudi Arabia, and made the pilgrimage to Mecca. His son was college-trained, and his daughter intended to be an electrical engineer. He showed me photographs of the family taken at various times.

'You see how he always takes the middle,' the son murmured sardonically. Across the way the *hagh* had built himself a brick house, with veranda, and we went up onto the roof to view things. An old man, very grave, and suffering from a severe cold, told me that the British had a camp nearby during the war. The *hagh*'s son translated.

'He says that he has heard the British were fair people.' The old man added something. 'He says that he has no first-hand knowledge of this, but he reports to you what he has heard.'

It stuck in my mind as the best of Egypt, that scrupulous honesty. It was uttered with a peasant calm hard to find in Cairo. Then there was a great shouting in the street below, and a more important villager summoned us to his house for tea. We sat in the reception room of quite a substantial house. Gilt chairs were ranged right round the wall. To my surprise, my host spoke excellent idiomatic English. I made some idle remark, to which he replied, suavely, 'Well, you must remember the lessons of your poet. Needs must when the devil drives.'

'Tonight I must drive to Alexandria.'

'Impossible. Not possible.'

'All the same I must.'

His face clouded, and he took what I said as a rebuff to his generosity. To bridge an awkward gap, I made some remark about having heard the crops were poor. When he looked up, there was a different man there: still speaking in excellent English, still polite, but somehow gone away.

'The tomatoes have been poor. It is Allah's judgement. If the crop is poor here, it is good somewhere else. You are not strictly allowed to be here, you know. Foreigners should not leave the road without permission.'

'I have gone to some trouble to get it.'

He shrugged. 'It is not for me to argue, therefore. But the next time you come to this village, you come to me. I am the man to see here, not this other family.'

'But I wished to meet a *hagh*, a pilgrim.'

'I am a *hagh*,' he shouted, outraged. 'I was also a parliamentary candidate.'

I did go to Alexandria, as a literary pilgrimage more than anything else. But the Alexandria of Cavafy has long since vanished. So has any honour or even memory of the Nile. Having spent so long in travelling, the greatest and longest river on earth does not rush out to greet the sea, and turn back its salt for a mile or so in triumph. But neither has it ended in defeat. I went to Alexandria, and I sat on a hotel balcony, overlooking a water-colour sea, and tried to find some summary version of the journey.

The Nile figures in the histories of all Western peoples. Its significance to Egypt used to be (perhaps still is) one of the great romances of geography taught to young children. No pictorial encyclopedia worth its salt would be without a photograph of a fellah working his shadoof, lifting water from the life-giving river. Nor do we count ourselves educated, in the temperate and niggardly north of Europe, if we cannot say *something* about dynastic Egypt. The exhibition of the funerary remains of Tutan-khamun, when they were toured a few years ago, was seen by millions. As were Sadat's assassination and the Arab-Israeli Wars. For British people, Suez was the virtual extinction of our nation as an influential foreign power.

But these things are to do with only the last 800 miles of a massive track across the surface of the earth, a river easily seen from the window of a spaceship with the naked eye. The wonder of the Nile is in its indifference to history, which it has so bountifully watered. At nightfall, in the grounds of the Alexandrian hotel, the palms tossed their heads against a Mediterranean breeze. And beyond them, for half the length of Africa, the moon was reflected in the waters of a river that flows as certainly and as surely as the earth revolves.

INDEX